BREAKOUT

BREAKOUT

FROM PRISON TO THE BIG LEAGUES

by Ron LeFlore with Jim Hawkins

AN ASSOCIATED FEATURES BOOK

HARPER & ROW, PUBLISHERS

NEW YORK

HAGERSTOWN

SAN FRANCISCO

LONDON

This is a true story. However, some of the names have been changed.

FIRST EDITION

Designed by Sidney Feinberg

Library of Congress Cataloging in Publication Data

LeFlore, Ron.
  Breakout.
  "An Associated Features book."
  1. LeFlore, Ron. 2. Baseball players—United
States—Biography. 3. Prisoners—United States—
Biography. I. Hawkins, Jim, joint author. II. Title.
GV865.L37A33 1978   796.357′092′4 [B]   77–3759
ISBN 0–06–012552–7

78 79 80 10 9 8 7 6 5 4 3 2 1

To the State Prison of Southern Michigan, where my new life began, and to my daughter, LaRonda, who has helped make that life meaningful

Ron LeFlore

And to Penny, who has always been there

Jim Hawkins

Contents

A section of photographs follows page 84

Acknowledgments

The authors wish to thank Jim Campbell, Hal Middlesworth, Lew Matlin, Bill Lajoie, Ed Katalinas, Hoot Evers, Ralph Houk, Bill Brown, and Gates Brown of the Detroit Tigers, who helped fill in the gaps; Bill Trippett, Jess Van Deusen and John Staten, who opened the doors of the State Prison of Southern Michigan to us; Mrs. Georgia LeFlore, Jimmy Butsicaris, and Jimmy Karalla, who shared their sides of the story; Bob Woolf, Zander and Phyllis Hollander, and Joe Vergara, who played their roles; and Penny, who did much more than merely type.

BREAKOUT

Prologue

Ron LeFlore sat on a stool in front of his cubicle in the visitors' clubhouse at Philadelphia's Veterans Stadium, leafing through the souvenir program he had found in his locker. He was barely aware of the words and pictures. He glanced at the clock. It was less than two hours until game time, and he felt the urge to be out on the field, to loosen up and get acquainted with the unfamiliar artificial turf.

He could hardly wait to step out of the dugout and look up into the stands, overflowing with nearly 64,000 people. He had never performed before a crowd this large and he wondered what it would be like. He looked forward to being introduced, to hearing his name called over the public address system, to trotting out in his grey doubleknit Detroit Tigers road uniform, and to standing on the foul line alongside his famous teammates. Would he be able to spot his mother and father in the crowd? He hoped so. He wanted very much to be able to share this moment with them.

He watched wide-eyed as a small group of well-dressed men slowly made its way along the row of lockers that lined the room, pausing for a few moments with each member of the American League All-Star team.

He was in awe of the scene and he didn't try to hide it.

Five years earlier, in July 1971, he had watched major league baseball's annual All-Star Game from the mess hall of the State Prison of Southern Michigan in Jackson, where he was serving a five-to-fifteen-year sentence for armed robbery. Some of the inmates had petitioned the warden for special permission to remain out of their cells past the 9:30 P.M. curfew in order to watch the game. It had been a rare treat.

He remembered seeing superstars Henry Aaron and Roberto Clemente play for the first time. He remembered watching Reggie Jackson of the Oakland A's bounce a stupendous home run off the light tower high above the rightfield roof at Tiger Stadium in that game. And he remembered wondering what it might be like to be a major league ballplayer, an All-Star.

He thought for sure he would never find out first hand. Convicted felons don't become big league ballplayers, much less All-Stars. (Especially a convicted felon who had never played baseball as a kid.) He was a branded young man with an illicit past, an uncertain future, and a number.

Now, incredibly, five years later to the day, on July 13, 1976, amid America's celebration of the 200th anniversary of its own emancipation, LeFlore was not only free but he was going to play in an All-Star Game. In fact he was the people's choice to lead off and play left field for the American League while millions of fans around the country—and in Jackson Prison—watched. The fact that nearly two million Americans had voted for him, Ron LeFlore, former thief, one-time drug addict, and ex-con, meant more to him than anything else.

"It means I'm a part of something I've never been a part of before," he said softly. "It means I'm a part of society now."

He was a professional ballplayer, and people were willing to accept him as that and to ignore his criminal background. Heralded as one of baseball's brightest new stars, he was the envy of nearly every young American boy. All his life Ron had wanted people to look up to him. At last they had a legitimate reason.

He had already established himself as the best base-stealer to wear a Detroit Tiger uniform since the immortal Ty Cobb. He had been Player of the Week and Player of the Month, and he had put together the longest hitting streak the American League had seen in twenty-seven years. Now, in only his second full season in the major leagues, he had been picked to participate in an annual exhibition that was synonymous with athletic excellence.

To think that until five years earlier, he had

never gripped a bat and hit a hard ball in his life. . . .

Finally the procession arrived in front of Ron's locker, and the smiling, balding man in the middle of the group extended his right hand. Ron grasped it firmly. The man congratulated Ron on his recent hitting streak and wished him continued good fortune. "We Michiganders have got to stick together," the man said with a broad grin.

LeFlore slumped back on his stool and drew a deep breath as Gerald R. Ford moved on, surrounded by his secret service entourage.

"How about that?" Ron sighed, grinning broadly himself. "The President of the United States knows who I am!"

Leading off the top half of the first inning, LeFlore singled sharply to left off San Diego's ace lefthander, Randy Jones, to begin the ball game. Standing on first base, Ron had to remind himself that it was really happening.

"There I was," he would recall later, "just three years out of prison, playing in my first All-Star Game, batting 1.000 against one of the best pitchers in baseball. It was the most thrilling thing that had ever happened to me."

He had come a long way from the dilapidated dope houses and dingy prison cell he once called home. A long, long way.

Jim Hawkins

Assault with Intent to Commit Robbery, Armed

1

It was my idea, so I suppose you could call me the ringleader. I might as well take most of the credit—I got most of the blame.

My best friend, Antoine, a fellow named Leroy, and I were hanging around O'Quinn's poolroom where we lived on Detroit's east side one night in January 1970—the 15th, I believe it was—when I suggested we pull a robbery. Just like that.

The three of us had been together the night before, snorting heroin in a dope house across the street, and Antoine and Leroy had spent all their money. They were broke. I had twenty or thirty dollars in my pocket and we all wanted to get high again, but I wasn't about to spend all my money on dope for them. A robbery seemed like the logical solution.

I've often wondered what would have happened if one of the other guys had said he didn't want to go through with it. After all, bad as we were, none of us had ever done anything quite that drastic before. If one of them had objected, we probably would have stopped right there and gone on to something else. In that case we never would have been caught that night. I wonder what the rest of my life would have been like then.

However, Antoine and Leroy were all for the idea, and there was certainly no way I was going to back out, even though I didn't actually need the money. I had my image to protect. If I had backed down, word would have gotten around that I was scared. By then I had become known as the best thief in the neighborhood, at least among guys my own age, and I was proud of that reputation. I wanted to keep it. I was nineteen years old, I had spent nineteen months in the state reformatory, and I was ready to branch out into bigger and better crimes.

We needed a gun, but none of the older guys in the poolroom would loan us one, so Leroy said he had a .22 caliber rifle we could use.

We were riding around in Leroy's '68 Mustang, trying to think of a place to rob, when I remembered a little neighborhood bar called Dee's. It was across the street from Chrysler's Mack Avenue Stamping Plant, and a lot of the workers from the factory cashed their paychecks there. Since it was Thursday, the day the guys got paid, I knew the place would have plenty of money on hand. I assured my friends it would be easy.

When we arrived there were a couple of people in the bar, drinking and visiting with the owner. We waited in the alley until they left and then the three of us charged in through the back door.

Since I was the gutsy one in the group, I was carrying

the rifle. I pointed it at the owner and shouted, "All right, this is a robbery! Don't nobody make any wrong moves, and nobody'll get hurt!"

Antoine and Leroy emptied the cash registers while I handled the owner and his wife. There wasn't any hassling; we weren't there to hurt anybody. I just told them to lay down on the floor.

I noticed a small safe in the rear of the bar, so I ordered the lady to open it. I grabbed a bag of money. I didn't know how much money was there—I hardly bothered to look inside. We dumped the money from the cash registers into the bag too, then told the people to lay back on the floor and not to move until we were gone. The whole thing only took about ten minutes. It was easy, just as I had promised.

I was the last one out and I still had the rifle pointed at the people, but I wasn't paying much attention to them. I wasn't even concerned when the lady reached for something as we were going out the door. I was only worried about getting away. I figured that even if they did have a silent burglar alarm to the police station, it was too late to stop us. As long as we got in and got out, I was sure we'd be okay.

Since it was Leroy's car, he was driving. He was about six-foot-four, and in his hurry to make the turn as he pulled out of the alley into the street his knee accidently bumped the light switch, shutting off the headlights. None of us noticed the lights go out. We were on Mack Avenue by then, under the streetlights, and we were only thinking about getting away as fast as we could.

Driving down the street with our lights out, trying to decide where we should go to split up the money, we spotted a police car coming toward us. The police blinked their headlights, and for the first time I got scared. I was sitting in the front seat with the rifle in my lap and I said to Leroy, "If those motherfuckers stop us I'm going to open fire—and you take off!"

I had my finger on the trigger ready to shoot, but the police were merely blinking their lights to let us know our lights were out. After they had passed, I suggested we stop at a dope house because the police would never expect three guys who had just pulled a robbery to be in a place like that. But the others insisted on going to Leroy's apartment about eight or ten blocks away. They wanted to split up the money immediately.

I convinced them we should wait until the next day. There was a heat vent in the apartment with a big chest in front of it, and we hid the money there. We had also stolen a .38 caliber pistol from the safe at the bar, so we stashed that in the heat vent too. Then I called a cab so Antoine and I could leave.

When the cabbie pulled up in front and blew his horn, I looked out and saw police cars all over the street. The police who had seen us in the vicinity of the robbery driving with our lights out must have taken our license number down, checked, and found the car belonged to Leroy.

When I saw the police outside, I didn't know what to do. We got a little panicky. I grabbed Antoine by the arm and said, "Let's you and me get the hell out of here!" Leroy's apartment was on the first floor, but there was an attic in the building, so Antoine and I went up there to hide. As soon as we got upstairs, we heard the police bust into Leroy's apartment. We heard some scuffling and the police saying something about a robbery. We knew it wouldn't be long before they'd come searching upstairs.

"I'm going downstairs and pretend I'm a resident here. I'll act like I wasn't involved and try to get away," I said. I took off my coat, my sweater, my shirt, and even my shoes. I went downstairs with just a pair of khaki pants on.

The door to Leroy's apartment was open; there must have been fifteen policemen inside. They had Leroy sitting in a chair with his hands cuffed behind him. As casually as I could, I looked in and said, "What's happening, man?"

"Who are you?" one of the officers snapped.

"I live upstairs," I replied. "I heard a lot of commotion and came down to see what was going on."

An officer pointed to Leroy and asked, "Do you know this guy?"

I nodded, "Yeah, I know him."

The police had gone upstairs by this time, and I knew they had found Antoine hiding in the attic because I could hear them dragging him down the stairs. I figured I had better get out of there right away.

"Well, I'm going to be going now Leroy," I said, trying my best to sound calm. I was so sure of myself; I really thought I was going to get away.

As I turned to go out the door, Leroy yelled, "He was with me, too!"

The police grabbed me and handcuffed me to a chair. I was hurt and mad and scared—all at the same time. We had vowed we would never tell on one another. If somebody got caught, it would be his responsibility—he would have to take all the weight. Yet there I was, caught, because one of my friends told on me.

We never did get to count the money we had taken. We didn't know until it was presented as evidence at our trials that we had stashed away nearly $35,000 in that heat vent.

When they took us downtown to Detroit Police Head-quarters, we were fingerprinted three or four times and mug shots were taken. After the detectives had questioned us, they put us in a line-up. Only Antoine and Leroy were picked out. The police didn't have anything on me except the fact that Leroy claimed I had been part of the heist. I was charged with armed robbery just the same, and my bail was set at $20,000. Then I was transferred to the Wayne County Jail, where I was fingerprinted and photographed all over again.

I knew my mother and father surely didn't have $20,000—they didn't even have a car. However, there were a couple of drug dealers in the neighborhood who probably would have been willing to put up my bail money. I thought about telling my parents to contact them but decided against it because I didn't want my mother and father to know the type of people I was involved with. They had been constantly on me about the company and the hours I was keeping—but they had no idea how bad that company really was. So I didn't mention my friends. I did ask my parents to try and get me a lawyer and a speedy trial.

In the county jail, an older prisoner advised me that the best thing to do when I went to arraignment would be to stand mute, which meant pleading not guilty. The police had separated Antoine, Leroy, and me in jail to prevent our agreeing on any one story. But when we went to arraignment, we were together for a few minutes in the bullpen. I told them I was going to stand mute and they should, too. Before the judge, Antoine and I stood mute, but Leroy pleaded guilty. He had already agreed to turn state's evidence and testify against us in exchange for a lighter sentence for himself.

We had separate trials. My lawyer and my mother both suggested I ask for a bench trial; they said if I did have to serve some time, I probably wouldn't get as much time from a judge as I would from a jury.

The judge knocked down the charge against me from armed robbery to assault with intent to commit robbery, armed—a lesser crime which carried a lighter sentence if the judge wanted to give it to you. When he dressed the words up a bit, the crime didn't sound so serious—even though it meant the same thing.

The judge talked to my lawyer and my parents. They all knew I was guilty, and I was advised to plead guilty to the lesser charge. I agreed.

At my sentencing the judge said he had intended to give me twenty-to-forty, since I was the one who carried the gun and that meant I was prepared to do serious bodily harm to anybody who got in our way. But, he said, because I was so young, and because my mother told him I was a pretty intelligent kid, and because he felt sorry for my parents, who were there crying during the trial, he had decided to give me no more than fifteen and no less than five years in the State Prison of Southern Michigan.

Antoine got three-to-five. Leroy was sentenced to thirty days in the Detroit House of Correction, plus five years' probation, because he testified against us.

I was bitter. I felt the judge had no right to put me away in prison. I didn't look upon myself as having done wrong— I looked upon myself as having been told on. I felt I had been screwed by society and by my friend.

The full impact of my sentence didn't really hit me until April 28, when the police took me to the state prison in Jackson, Michigan, about seventy-five miles west of Detroit.

Riding along Interstate 94 in a police station wagon with a couple of other prisoners, I suddenly felt sick to my stomach. The windows were barred, I was handcuffed, I had heavy belly chains around me—I was nineteen years old and considered a hardened criminal. I wasn't thinking about being able to get out of prison in five years; I figured I was going to have to serve the full fifteen.

Then I saw the prison. It was huge, at least a city block long in each direction, and there was a high, red brick wall around it. There seemed to be a dark rain cloud hanging over the whole place. It looked like something straight out of a nightmare.

My fists were clenched and I could feel myself sweating. "Be strong," I told myself, "don't cry."

They took us inside to the reception area. And I saw the cells. As far as I could see, there was nothing but cells. Five tiers of cells. And outside the walkways, in front of the cells, there was a heavy black wire screen from the floor to the ceiling. One of the guards said that was to prevent the inmates from committing suicide by jumping off the walkways.

I looked at that huge cell block and that screen and, for the first time since I had been arrested, I broke down. I didn't feel very tough, or very clever, or very grown up. I kept asking myself, "How am I ever going to be able to do all that time in a place like this?"

At that moment my whole life seemed over.

If You Were Lucky, You Survived

2

I was a typical kid in many ways. I loved to get into mischief with my friends. If somebody in the neighborhood had a cherry tree in the back yard, we'd climb the tree and steal the cherries. If somebody had sheets hanging on the clothes line, we would snatch them down. And we'd run.

I always could run pretty fast. I got a lot of practice running from the police, even when I was young. I liked to throw rocks at police cars, trying to break their windows. When policemen rode down the street on motorcycles, I'd try to throw sticks through the spokes to make them fall. That was a lot of fun. And it was typical of the way most people in the neighborhood felt about the police.

Our neighborhood was different from most neighborhoods. Instead of parks and playgrounds and pretty little houses with white picket fences, we had prostitutes and drug addicts and dope houses on nearly every block.

While kids growing up in other neighborhoods were

13

playing baseball and football and basketball, I was sneaking around the streets, stealing whatever I could. While other kids were in school studying algebra and geography, I was standing on the corner, drinking wine and smoking grass. While other kids were home with their parents in the evening, watching TV, I was hanging around dope houses or selling speed and stolen clothes to prostitutes and pimps. That was the way I grew up. That's not a complaint and it's not an excuse. That's just the way it was.

Except for a few white people, our neighborhood was black. However, that wasn't the reason it was so bad. There were a lot of other all-black neighborhoods in the City of Detroit where kids enjoyed what are generally considered normal childhoods.

Traditionally the east side of Detroit, where I was born and raised, has always been the toughest part of town. The east side has always had a lot of prostitution and drugs and underworld activity. People there tend to be blue-collar, working-class people, if they have jobs at all.

Blacks living on the west side have more money; they also have baseball fields and parks for recreation. We didn't have any facilities like that. Kids on the west side played baseball; kids on the east side had other things in mind. If you were lucky, you survived.

Our neighborhood was the worst. It was truly crime-infested. Prostitution, robbery, drugs, murder—everything you could possibly think of was going on in the six or seven block area near where we lived. The favorite pastime of the community was committing crimes; it was the "in" thing to do.

From the time I was small I saw all that going on and assumed that was the way the world was—the way things were supposed to be. That was all I knew. When you're brought up in a ghetto, you're really confined to that certain area. My parents didn't have enough money to take us on picnics, to amusement parks, or to fairs. We didn't have a car. When I was coming up, I didn't know the suburbs existed. I didn't know we lived in a slum; I didn't know what a ghetto was. I didn't even realize that my parents were poor. That was the only side of life I saw, so I thought that was the way all life was. Everyone else was committing crimes and getting away with them, so I assumed I could commit crimes and get away with them too.

It was no big deal when I stole from a store or let a prostitute know the police were in the area. I knew who the drug addicts in the neighborhood were and where they got their drugs. I took all that for granted, and I was only in grade school.

I stole some of my mother's cigarettes and started smoking when I was nine because the guys I was running around with smoked. I started drinking wine when I was eleven because I saw the older kids standing on the corner drinking wine. I started smoking marijuana when I was thirteen because everybody started smoking marijuana when they turned thirteen. I began using hard drugs when I was fifteen because all the older kids used them, and I thought that was the grown-up thing to do.

We hardly played any sports. I did play basketball on the church team in the YMCA League a couple of years, and sometimes we would get together makeshift football or stickball teams and play in the alley or street. That was about it. We never had gloves or real bats. We used an old mop handle or a broomstick and a rubber ball. Sneaking around the streets, seeing what we could get away with, appealed to us more than sports.

My parents were from Memphis, Tennessee. Actually

my father, John, was born in Mississippi, but he was raised in Memphis and that was where he met my mother, Georgia. They moved to Detroit in 1943 and my father got a job in an auto factory. Seven years later, on June 16, 1950, I was born.

People always ask me what nationality LeFlore is. It's French. I'm told my great great grandfather was French and Indian.

I had three brothers, but two of them are now dead. My oldest brother, Harry, died in 1961, when I was eleven. A lightweight boxer who was considered a good prospect, he suffered a head injury and wouldn't listen when the doctors told him he should quit fighting. He hit his head on a post in the ring in his third professional fight and died.

My younger brother, Gerald, was shot and killed on April 23, 1976. I knew he was involved in drugs; my parents and I had tried to help him. We used to fight all the time when we were kids, but we were very close. It really hurt me when he was killed.

My other older brother, Marvin, lives in California. I see him whenever the Tigers play on the West Coast, and he always comes home for the holidays. He's in the real estate business. But I'm not as close to him as I was to Gerald.

My mother and father always tried to do what was best for us boys to make us grow up right. They wanted us to do well in school so we could establish ourselves as respectable citizens. They were constantly after my brothers and me to stay with the books and study. They didn't have many opportunities when they were coming up, and they wanted us to grow up and have all the things they never had.

It was hard for them. Although my father was working

in an auto factory, he wasn't making enough money to take us to a lot of places or to do things that other fathers did with their sons. Much of the time while I was growing up my mother was working, too. They tried to keep an eye on us as best they could.

One night I was at a friend's house real late and my father came after me. Several prostitutes were living in that house, and my parents had told me they didn't want me hanging around there. But I sneaked over anyway because I liked to look at all the pretty girls. I knew my father was furious when I heard him hollering outside the front door. I told my friends to tell him I wasn't there. My father didn't believe them. He gathered up some paper and some debris from the yard and started a fire right on the front porch. It probably wasn't big enough to burn the house down, but it sure made me come out in a hurry.

Most of the time, though, my father was gone. He had a drinking problem. What little extra money he did have he spent on alcohol. I know he loved us. Sometimes he'd take us boys out in the back yard to play—but usually when he came home he was so drunk he went right to bed. Maybe if he had done more things with me, I wouldn't have gotten into trouble. I don't know.

I do know that by the time I was nine or ten I didn't care if my parents took me anywhere. I preferred to be with friends. With them I knew I could do anything I wanted to do—steal or smoke cigarettes—without having to worry about anyone yelling at me. My parents never would let me do the things I really wanted to do.

Whenever I did something wrong and was caught red-handed, I got spanked. But I could usually tell my parents a good lie and get away with it, even when I was little. As

I got older, I got better and better at it. They never knew when I was lying. By the time I got to high school, my mother and father had no idea what I was doing. And I was doing a lot.

Dumbo, Miss Price, and Emma Mae

"I didn't know he was running the streets and getting into trouble," maintains Ron's mother, Mrs. Georgia LeFlore. "I'd like to have died when he went to prison.

"We did the best we could, my husband and I. But when you can't get the decent jobs that pay you the right amount of money—it takes two paychecks to raise children—and when two people are working, trying to make things go, it's tough. We had a pretty well-rounded family. The children had a lot of love and understanding. They could always come to me and talk to me, and I could always understand their problems. You would think things like that would mean a lot to a child.

"We were church people. I think our kids were the only kids on the block who went to church. I was in contact with their teachers at school all the time, I

19

was in the PTA, I was involved in different activities at the school. I paid attention to my children.

"Ronald wasn't an arrogant child. He always got good marks in school; he got good cards. I don't see how, going to church, and being a good student, a child could get into so much trouble.

"It just shows you: You don't even know your own children. You think you do, but you don't."

I always was very bold, even as a little boy. When I was in the first grade my mother made me wear short pants to school, but I thought only girls wore shorts and I started crying. I didn't want my friends to laugh at me. I made up my mind that if I had to wear those pants, I wasn't going to school.

Along the way there was an old garage with a storage shed attached, so I cut through the alley, climbed into that shed, and went to sleep. At noon I went home and ate lunch as if I had been in school all morning, then went back to the shed and waited until school got out.

The teacher knew my mother and called to find out why I wasn't in school. When I got home my mother asked, "What did you do in school today?" I said I wasn't feeling well so I didn't do anything. She swatted me and said, "You're telling stories."

The next day my mother took me to school. She made me wear short pants again, too. She plucked a switch off a tree on the way and then spanked me in class in front of my friends. That cured me of skipping school for a while. But I don't think many six-year-olds would even have had the nerve to try something like that.

I was good in school at first. I was smart. But I was always busy looking up under the little girls' dresses. I liked to cheat, too, even though I didn't need to. Finally my second grade teacher moved me next to her desk, right by the blackboard, so I couldn't look up under the little girls' dresses or cheat anymore.

My father was an avid baseball fan—he loved the New York Yankees—and once or twice a year, when the Yankees came to Detroit, he would take us kids to Tiger Stadium to see a ball game. We lived about fifteen minutes from the ball park.

I can remember sitting in the bleachers at Tiger Stadium, but I can't remember much about the ballplayers. I just wasn't interested. The only player I remember is Don Mossi, a relief pitcher with the Tigers. And all I remember about him were his big ears. I called Don Mossi "Dumbo" because he looked like Dumbo the Elephant on the Mickey Mouse show on TV. Whenever my father saw a picture of Don Mossi in the paper he'd ask, "Who's that?" I'd laugh and say, "That's Dumbo!"

I didn't have any heroes among the ballplayers. My father and mother used to talk about Willie Mays and, of course, about the Yankees, but I didn't pay any attention. I didn't collect baseball cards or try to get autographs when we went to the ball park. I never read the sports pages. I never heard of guys like Ted Williams or Stan Musial or Roberto Clemente. I didn't even watch baseball on TV. The only sport I watched was football—and my father never took me to a football game.

There was an old warehouse in the neighborhood, with a parking lot alongside, and once in a while we would go there and hit a ball against the building. There were some lines on the side of the building, and if we hit the ball over a certain line we said it was a single, a double, a triple, or a home run. Other than that I didn't play much baseball. I didn't like the game.

When I was eight I joined the Boy Scouts. You were supposed to be ten to get in, but I lied about my age. My parents wanted me to get into the Cub Scouts, but I thought the Cub Scout uniforms looked sissy-ish. The Boy Scouts had a real nice looking Army patch on their uniforms. Besides, a few of my friends were already in the Boy Scouts, and I wanted to be with them. I never studied my Boy Scout manual though, and I never learned to tie all those different knots. After a couple of years I lost interest and quit.

I got interested in girls earlier than guys usually do, probably because of the neighborhood. With all those prostitutes around, kids couldn't help but think about sex.

When I was ten years old I had a girl friend, Emma Mae, who lived across the street. I was in love! She was a couple of years older, and we would stand alongside her house at night, kissing and rubbing up against each other. She started messing with an older guy and eventually became a prostitute. That broke my heart. I told myself I wasn't ever going to fall in love again.

A friend had an older sister named Veronica whom I used to like, too. She was seventeen or eighteen and wouldn't have anything to do with me because I was only eleven. But she had big tits and a nice firm butt, and whenever I was over there I'd grab her tittie or grab her butt. She would chase me all over the house. I really thought I was doing something grown-up.

I remember the first sex I had. I was thrilled about it. I was twelve years old; the girl was seventeen. She was a prostitute who belonged to a pimp I knew. I did the guy a little favor one day and he told her to make love with me. Just like that. So she did. I couldn't wait to tell all my friends about it. None of them believed me.

Ron's young friends found many of the things he did as a kid a bit unbelievable.

"Ronald was always the exception to the rule," recalls twenty-six-year-old Calvin Qualls, who lived two doors away from Ron when they were growing up. "He could do anything anyone else could do, and he could do it three or four times better. He could do it long before anyone else was old enough to try, too. He was something else. He and his brother Gerald were the best athletes in the neighborhood.

"There was nothing he couldn't do well. He was the best around—at everything—football, basketball, fighting, you name it. Everybody looked up to him.

"Ronald could have been the first black hockey player, I swear he could," continues Qualls. "Blacks don't mess with ice skates, but one winter it seemed like everybody got skates for Christmas. We all went to the Salvation Army and got some old pads and stuff, and we flooded the alley out back of our house and made a skating rink. We were out there every day for a while, trying to play hockey. But Ronald was the only one who could skate. And he had never done it before, either."

Although Qualls had two older brothers, he frequently turned to Ron, who was two years older, when he found himself in trouble.

"He was like an older brother to me," says

Qualls. "When my brothers weren't around and I'd get beat up, I used to run crying to Ronald. And he'd take care of me. There weren't many people who wanted to fight Ronald.

"One time a guy named Sylvester jumped on me and beat me up. My brothers weren't home, so I found Ronald and told him what had happened. He said we'd go get the guy. As we were walking down the alley, Ronald said, 'We're going to be fighting, but when I get ready to hurt him, I'm going to wink my eye.'

"When we found Sylvester, Ronald jumped on him and they started fighting. They fought for, I'd say, three or four minutes. Then Ronald winked his eye. And that was practically the end of the fight. After that, I didn't have any more trouble with Sylvester."

After dark, young Ron and his friends amused themselves by roller-skating down the middle of Van Dyke Avenue, a busy, main thoroughfare between downtown Detroit and the suburbs, dodging cars as they raced to see who would finish first. More often than not the winner was Ron.

Not satisfied with being recognized as the fastest runner in the neighborhood, twelve-year-old Ron challenged Calvin Qualls's older brother Godfrey to a race in the alley one afternoon—while Godfrey was driving his Chrysler New Yorker.

At twenty miles an hour, according to Ron, the two were still fender-to-shoulder.

When he became bored racing cars and roller-skating down the middle of the street, Ron *made up a new game. He called it simply "the running game."*

"We'd wait until it got dark, pitch-black at night," recalls Calvin Qualls. "Then one person would be it, and he'd start chasing everyone else in the neighborhood. We'd climb up on the garages and jump from garage to garage to get away. Sometimes we'd go a whole block like that before we got back down on the ground.

"It was dark, so sometimes guys would fall and get hurt. And once you got caught you had to help catch the rest. But Ronald was always the last one to get caught. Who else but Ronald would ever think of a game like that?"

I got into a lot of fights in school. It seemed like I was always getting kicked out for fighting. I went to nine different schools before I finally quit. Public school, Catholic school, reform school—I went to them all.

In the fourth grade I was in love with my teacher, Miss Price. I loved being in her class. My problem was that I wouldn't pay attention to what she was saying. I was always too busy looking at her legs or at how pretty she was.

One day during a spelling test I cheated because I hadn't studied. I wrote the words on my desk, and when they passed out the paper I slipped the spelling sheet over them.

Marie, the girl next to me, saw me cheating and told the teacher. I got a failing grade on the test and knew I was in for a whipping when I got home. I told Marie I was going to beat her up after school for getting me in trouble.

I was a safety patrol boy at the time, and when Marie

came out the door I left my corner post and clobbered her. For that I got kicked out of Jones Elementary School.

I transferred to Joyce Elementary School and got into a fight there, too. We were playing a game called "pom-pom," in which the object was to try to tag everybody, when I accidentally ran into a kid named Marvin Wilson and knocked him down. He was supposed to be the toughest kid in the school, and right away he wanted to fight. I didn't want to get kicked out of another school so soon, so I backed off. He pulled a drawing compass on me, though, and threatened to stab me with it. I pointed my finger in his face and shouted, "I'll get you after school for that."

When school got out I went looking for him and caught up with him about three blocks away. I socked him in the eye with my first punch and knocked him down. I jumped on top of him, pinned his arms with my knees, and began beating his face. The football coach from a Catholic school nearby broke up the fight, but as soon as we were out of his sight I jumped on Marvin Wilson again. This time he broke loose and belted me in the jaw. It was the first time he had hit me, and it made me so mad I busted his nose. He went home and told his mother, so I was expelled again. My mother had to plead with the principal to get me reinstated.

In spite of my fighting I was smart enough to be double-promoted once. We were on the semester system, and I went from the second semester of the sixth grade to the second semester of the seventh grade. The other kids couldn't understand how I could get so many As and Bs when I hardly ever studied. The work always seemed easy for me; I could pick things up quickly. Of course I did a lot of cheating to get those As and Bs, too.

When I got to junior high school, my attitude got even

worse. I started skipping school more and more. I usually passed the tests even if I didn't study very much; I did just enough work to get by.

One of the girls who worked in the school office liked me, so she stole a blank report card for me and stamped it. I just filled in my own grades and took the card home so my parents wouldn't know how much school I was skipping or how bad my marks really were. A friend forged my mother's signature on my real report card and I returned that one to the school. It worked so well that I decided to handle my report cards that way from then on.

Eventually I was kicked out of junior high for stealing another guy's lunch card. Kids from families on welfare were eligible for a special card that allowed them to eat for free in the school cafeteria. We weren't on welfare at the time, so I didn't have a card, but I stole one from the home-room teacher's desk and used it. Somebody told on me, and since I had already been in so much trouble for fighting and skipping school I was expelled.

This time I was sent to A. L. Holmes, a special school for delinquent boys. It wasn't actually a reform school—I still lived at home—but kids who were sent there usually went right on to reform school and then to prison as they got older.

The staff at the school couldn't figure me out. They couldn't understand why I had been getting into so much trouble. The psychiatrist said I had a little inferiority complex—I always wanted to be better than everybody else at whatever I did—but other than that there was nothing wrong with me. The teachers were amazed because I walked right in and did junior high school work. I got all As and Bs; they couldn't believe it. They didn't think I belonged in a school like that. I only did my work because I wanted to get out. Six months later I did.

When I got to high school I made up my mind I was going to be a football player. Even though I hadn't actually played much, I enjoyed the game because it was rough and there was a lot of contact. I was determined to go to school and do my work so I could play football. I was going to win a scholarship, go to college, and then, to the National Football League, where I'd be a star running back like my idol, Jim Brown.

If I had listened to my parents, kept my head straight, and stuck with the books, I would have made it, too. I know I would. I was that good.

Though we weren't Catholic, I enrolled at a Catholic school, St. Rose High, because they had a good football program. I had never played organized football, and I was a little leery when I showed up for practice the first day and saw all those big linemen. I wasn't used to playing with guys that big. I had only played little pick-up games in the street or on an empty lot, where we never wore pads or equipment. We played in sweatshirts and tennis shoes, and we called time-out every time a car came.

Still, I was used to playing against kids who had played football in high school—even a few who had gone on to college. And I had run through, around, and over those guys. I figured that if I could play with them, there was nothing a player in an organized high school game could possibly do to me.

I was only five-foot-nine and about 155 pounds, but I was quick. The upper part of my body was small, but my legs were big and strong. I had good speed, very good balance, and good lateral movements. I soon discovered I was faster than anyone else on the team. During practice I never got tackled in the backfield for a loss. Whenever a guy grabbed me I broke loose. I wasn't the type of runner who tippy-toed along; I charged guys.

Because I was a freshman I started on the junior varsity, which scrimmaged against the varsity every day. The junior varsity coach would select his best players for the scrimmage, and I was always one of the guys picked. I always did well, too. Just before the regular season opened I was promoted to the varsity. The coach was talking about making me one of his starting running backs, and I began thinking I could be All-City, maybe even All-America in high school.

A freshman really had to be an exceptional athlete to make varsity, so I had a tougher time in practice than the guys who were already on the team. I knew they were punishing me to see how strong I was and how much guts I had. I was sore every night, but I took it all in stride.

One day in practice we were having a three-on-one drill, where one defensive player is supposed to break through two blockers and tackle the quarterback. When my turn came to be the defensive player I bolted through the two linemen and grabbed the quarterback. As we went down I had my left shoulder buried in his gut. The two linemen were pissed off because I made them look bad, so both of them piled on top of us. I felt a severe pain shoot through the whole left side of my body. When I got up my arm and shoulder were throbbing and I told the coach I was hurt.

"There ain't a fuckin' thing wrong with you!" he screamed. "Get back out there and get to that quarterback again!"

My arm was really aching, but I trotted back out on the

field. As soon as the ball was snapped one of the linemen smacked my arm and I collapsed in pain.

The coach still thought I was shamming and accused me of not hustling. "My arm really hurts," I insisted. I was practically crying. But he didn't believe me. After practice I couldn't even take my shoulder pads off—they had to cut them away. When he saw that, the coach came over and said he was sorry. The doctor told me I had broken the growth bone in my left shoulder.

I never did get to play in an actual football game. I couldn't even go to school for awhile because of my shoulder, and I fell way behind in my studies. When I couldn't play football I began to drift away—from sports, school, my family, from everything except the streets.

When I went back to school they told me I would be eligible to play basketball the last half of the season, if I could catch up on my class work by the time the second quarter started. I began practicing basketball every night, becoming so involved in that game that I shied away from the books even more. We practiced until seven o'clock at night. I was usually so tired when I got home that I ate and went right to bed. I really wanted to play basketball, but I had lost all interest in doing my school work. I fell so far behind that I knew I could never catch up, and I dropped out of St. Rose High before they could expel me.

That meant I had to go to public school. I wanted to go to Northeastern High because they had the best basketball team. We didn't live in that area, so I lied about my address when I went to the school to register. I attended Northeastern for only a month before I was kicked out for skipping classes. The principal told me I'd have to bring my mother to school in order to get back in. I knew if I did that, they'd find out I had lied about my address and I'd get kicked out anyway.

I decided to transfer to Eastern High, where I was supposed to have gone in the first place. I persuaded a prostitute to pose as my mother and enroll me at Eastern, telling them we had just moved into the neighborhood.

I went out for basketball at Eastern, too, and after a couple of weeks the coach was talking about starting me at forward. Even though I was only five-foot-nine, I was consistently able to outjump guys who were six-foot-two and six-foot-three. I was quicker than most of the other guys on the team, I had a decent jump shot, and I could dunk the ball frontward and backward, with one hand or two.

As much as I enjoyed playing basketball, I didn't want to go to school. I thought being in class was too time-consuming, too boring. I was slightly ahead of most of the other kids when I first went to Eastern because of what I had learned at St. Rose, but again I did only enough work to get by. I frequently put my head down on my desk in class and went to sleep because I simply wasn't interested.

I began cutting a few classes and hanging around the pizza parlor across the street from the school. Pretty soon, instead of skipping one or two classes, I was staying out all day. We'd drink wine or stand around the poolroom and bullshit. When school let out at 3:30, I'd go inside for basketball practice. I really thought I was slick.

One day during practice the coach called me aside and said, "I've seen you across the street during school hours. What were you doing out there?" I told him those were my study hall periods and I had all my work done. He checked my schedule and the next day he yelled at me in front of the whole team. "Those weren't your study hall periods," he shouted, "you were skipping school! It had better not happen again!"

I kept right on skipping. I was so cocky I even skipped health class—and my health class teacher was the basketball coach. I had heard of guys who were dumb in the books and who passed anyway because they were athletes, and I wanted those benefits myself. I figured the coach would pass me no matter what because he wanted me to play basketball.

This coach wasn't like that; he wanted his athletes to study. He liked the All-American boy types—and that certainly wasn't me. So he kicked me off the team. The following year, in the tenth grade, I dropped out of school completely. I had noticed that most of the guys who hung around the poolroom didn't work, didn't go to school, and didn't seem to have a care in the world. That was the life for me.

The Invisible Man

4

Stealing was my specialty. As far back as I can remember, I was stealing things and getting away with it. Whenever the other kids didn't want to steal something I would do it. And I wouldn't get caught. I seemed to have more nerve than anyone else. I was a real daredevil.

Everytime I went into a store I would steal something, even if it was only a rubber ball or one of those ten-cent miniature pies, just to show the other kids I could do it. Sometimes I would steal for the thrill of it. I got away with so much stuff that I began to believe I couldn't get caught. Usually everything I did was right out in the open, too. I thought I was The Invisible Man.

I liked people to look up to me—maybe that was one reason I stole so much when I was a kid. In school, instead of thinking about my books, I was constantly thinking about stealing, about being a better thief than any of the guys I grew up with. And I think I accomplished that. I was doing things that other kids my age—even in our neighborhood, bad as it was—didn't dream of doing. A lot of kids wanted to hang around me because I was so bold and gutsy. I liked that, and I would take kids with me and show them how to steal. But I always had to be the one to do it; it made me feel important. Even some of the older kids looked up to me because I was getting away with so much. That made me feel especially proud. I always wanted people to believe I was better than they were, whether we were playing stick-ball in the street or stealing. I was always competitive, and I didn't want people to beat me at anything. I had to be first.

When I was ten I began stealing from the neighborhood A&P where I worked on weekends. (I carried groceries home for people for whatever tips they might give me.) I hung around the store so much the manager and the clerks got accustomed to seeing me, and I became so trusted there that it was easy prey for me.

One night, while I was in the rear of the store helping the manager, Mr. Richardson, sweep up, I unlocked the back door. After everyone had left I sneaked back in with some friends and we stole all the steaks and wine we could carry. We sold them around the neighborhood to prostitutes and drunks. At Christmas I put a dozen hams in a couple of big grocery bags, placed the bags in a shopping cart, and walked out the front door—right past the cashiers, past the manager, past the security guard, past everybody. Nobody said a word. I sold some of the hams and I took a couple of them home to my mother. I told her the manager of the A&P had given them to me for helping him sweep up. That was the only time my parents ever benefited from anything I stole.

When I was twelve my mother got me a paper route.

My father had always said he didn't want me to work while I was growing up—he wanted me to go to school and try to make something of myself. However, my mother thought I should get in the habit of earning my own money. She even helped me deliver the papers. It wasn't a real newspaper, just one of those little advertising papers that the stores put out once a week. It was free to the customers, but I got paid for delivering four hundred of them. That job didn't last very long. It was hard work. Stealing was much easier.

One Saturday afternoon shortly after I quit my paper route, I noticed one of the cashiers in the A&P placing the money from her register into two brown envelopes. She pushed the envelopes through a slit into a drawer underneath the counter and went to lunch.

I knew the drawer was locked. There was one under each checkout counter, and I had seen Mr. Richardson open them after closing time and take money out. I went outside, found a stick, and put a wad of bubble gum on the end of it. The register across the aisle was still open for business, and there was a long line of people at that counter waiting to pay for their groceries. That didn't stop me.

I dropped down on my hands and knees behind the counter, poked the stick through the slit into the drawer, and fished around until I felt an envelope. I jabbed it so the gum would stick and hauled the envelope out. I shoved it down inside my shirt. My heart was really pounding. When I looked around, though, nobody was paying any attention to me. If the other cashier or any of the customers at the other counter had looked over, they would have seen me for sure. But none of them did.

So I poked the stick into the drawer again and fished the other envelope out. I shoved that inside my shirt too and ran home. My mother and father weren't there, so I went into the basement and ripped open the envelopes. As soon as I began counting the money, I knew I'd made quite a haul. I called to my little brother Gerald and shouted, "We're rich! We're rich!" There was about $1,500 lying on the basement floor. I was only twelve years old.

I made my brother promise he wouldn't tell, then the two of us went downtown and bought a bunch of clothes. I gave some away to my friends, along with some money. But I didn't give anything to my parents because I knew I'd get a whipping if they found out. You'd think a twelve-year-old would have been afraid, hiding that much money from his parents, but it didn't faze me at all.

On one occasion I did get caught—trying to steal some tools from a hardware store. The officers at the Youth Bureau had a big paddle they called "the Board of Education." As soon as they started spanking me I started confessing, and I couldn't stop. I told them about all the different things I had stolen—even the $1,500 from the A&P.

The officers took me home to tell my parents and then they took me to the A&P to face the manager, Mr. Richardson. But that was all they did. I don't think they really believed a kid my age could steal that much money. Guys who were bigger and older couldn't steal that much unless they used a gun.

Most of the time stealing was easy for me, and one crime led to another. One Saturday night a group of us, armed with only a big stick, broke into a drug store and emptied the cash register. We got about $300, mostly in change. We took the money to a vacant lot and divided it up, a dollar at a time, until the police came and we had to run. The next day we all went to Edgewater Park, an amusement park on Detroit's west side. We spent every dime we had stolen the night before on candy and games and rides. In fact, we forgot to save money for the bus ride home.

While standing around wondering what to do, I saw a lady go upstairs to the park administration office with a big bag under her arm. When she came back down a few minutes later she didn't have the bag. I thought it might have been full of money, so I went up the stairs to scout around. The office door was locked. I borrowed a fingernail file from one of my friends, and after some jiggling and turning of the file in the lock, the door opened. I don't know how—I'd never picked a lock before in my life. I just did what I had seen crooks do on TV, and I guess I was lucky.

The office was empty except for a big safe, which was unlocked. There were two bags of money inside, one filled with change and the other with dollar bills. I stuffed the bills in my pockets and took the bag full of change downstairs for my brother and my friends. I told myself that if anybody stopped me going down the stairs, I would say I was looking for the bathroom. I don't know whether it would have worked or not. As usual, nobody noticed me.

I borrowed a jacket from one of the guys, placed it over my shoulder to hide the money, and headed for the front gate. The change was jingling quite a bit, and I was afraid the policeman who stood near the gate might be suspicious. So I sent my brother and another guy ahead to fake a fight. While the police were busy breaking them up, I walked out the gate. When we got on the bus we all sat in the big seat at the back and dumped the change out right there on the seat. The bus was fairly crowded, and any one of those people could have been an off-duty policeman, but we didn't think about that. We never considered the possibility of getting caught. We simply dumped that change out on the seat—there was close to $300—and sat in the bus dividing it up. We were proud of ourselves because we had gotten our hands on all that money. (I never mentioned the dollar bills in my pants pockets.)

On another occasion when I needed money I called a lady named Liz, who lived in our neighborhood and was involved in the numbers racket. I asked her to loan me some money so I could go to a movie. When she refused I decided to get even and called the police. I don't know whether the people in the house got a tip that the police were coming or not, but they all ran out the back door moments before the police arrived. The police knocked on the front door, but when nobody answered they left. As soon as they had gone, I went in the back door and searched until I found a shoe box full of numbers slips and money.

I rounded up some of my friends, and we went to a sporting goods store to spend the money. We were going to buy equipment and uniforms and form a softball team called the East Side Upsetters. Along the way we got to thinking that we could have a softball team, but we wouldn't have anybody to play because we'd be the only team in the neighborhood. We bought a few gloves instead, and we played among ourselves the rest of the afternoon. That was the only glove I ever owned as a kid.

Three or four times I was picked up by the police for stealing and hauled down to the Youth Bureau. They would keep me overnight, or sometimes for a couple of days, until my parents came to get me. My father would get mad and scream, "I ain't coming down to get you, and I'm going to stop your mother from coming, too!" But I knew my mother would always come. My father usually came, too.

The juvenile officers threatened to send me to reform school. But I was still going to school at the time, so I knew I didn't have to worry about that. They don't send you to reform school as long as you're still attending regular school. They were just trying to scare me.

Actually the juvenile officers stuck up for me most of the time because they didn't think I was really a bad kid. One of the officers lived down the street from us, and he stopped by the house once in a while just to talk. Of course he had no idea of the things I was doing; I only got caught for the little crimes.

When I was thirteen they put me on juvenile probation for robbing a paper boy. I needed some money so I grabbed a kid and took his collection money. He didn't know me, but someone who saw me did and told the police.

The probation officer came out to our house once a month to ask my mother how I was doing in school and how I was behaving. He had given me a curfew; I was supposed to be in the house every night at six o'clock. But there wasn't any sense in that, especially in the summertime, so my mother let me stay out. The probation officer always called before he came over, and my mother would get word to me, wherever I was, to come right home. Somehow it seemed I was always home when the probation officer stopped by.

At fourteen I began sneaking out of the house at night after my parents thought I was asleep. My mother was working afternoons and when she got home she always peeked in the bedroom where Gerald and I slept to make sure we were okay. She never turned on the light because she assumed we were asleep. I would stuff a couple of pillows under my blanket to make it look like I was there and then climb out the bedroom window. Our bedroom was right over the front porch; it was an easy jump from the roof of the porch to the ground. I was like Batman—by the time my mother looked in the door, I'd be long gone. Sometimes I'd stay out all night.

I began hanging around the poolroom even though I was underage. Some of the guys I was running with were a few years older, and the owner of the poolroom must have thought I was the same age. Or maybe he didn't care.

The older guys let me hang around because I was easygoing and a good stealer. As long as I didn't get in the way or run my mouth off they'd let me run with them. I kept my eyes and ears open and picked up a lot.

I saw the flashy clothes they were wearing and I wanted clothes like that. They had money and I wanted that. Some of them had big cars, so I wanted one too. It didn't matter that they were four or five years older than I was—I wanted to have everything they had, right then. I felt grown up.

I decided I was going to be a pimp when I got older. When guys came around the neighborhood looking for prostitutes, my friends and I would pretend we were leading them to a houseful of girls, then we'd threaten them and take their money. It wasn't that I was a bully or a tough guy; I got along with almost everybody on the streets. That was just one more thing I could do and get away with.

I enjoyed hanging around prostitutes because they talked hip all the time. It was a totally different environment from what I was accustomed to at home, and I liked it. I decided that was the way I wanted to live. Later I changed my mind and decided I was going to be a drug dealer; I figured I could make more money doing that. I lost all interest in sports and I resented everything connected with school.

Some of the older guys belonged to gangs like the Shakers and the Bean Boys. I didn't think it was necessary to join one because I knew almost everybody in the neighborhood. Besides, I was never the type of person who enjoyed going out with ten guys and beating up two or three guys just for the hell of it. That didn't make sense to me. I was more interested in stealing money or stealing things that I could sell to get money. Those of us who ran around together didn't consider ourselves a gang. We were just out on the streets, trying to have a little fun.

Once in a while in the summer we played basketball on the school grounds at night. The playground was lighted, so we would get high on grass or wine, then go over there around midnight and shoot baskets until morning. Or we might just sit on the playground and bullshit. Stroh's Brewery was nearby, and we knew where they parked the trucks that were loaded and ready to go out the next morning. It was easy for us to jump the fence and steal a couple of cases of beer. We'd sit all night drinking beer, smoking cigarettes, smoking grass, and enjoying ourselves. The police hardly ever came around that late, and if they did, we could always spot them before they got close.

Usually, though, we were looking for something to steal. We weren't very well organized, and most of our crimes were spur of the moment things. One night we broke into a Sears & Roebuck store through a basement window, determined to steal some TV and stereo sets. We didn't have a car or a truck; none of us was even old enough to drive. We were going to carry as much stuff as we could as far as we could. We had the boxes all lined up, ready to go, but we couldn't get the back door of the store open and we couldn't get the boxes out through the basement window. So we grabbed all the clothes we could carry and hauled them out the way we came in.

I was always in charge, no matter what we did. Since I was the gutsy one in the group, I got to keep the most money. But that wasn't why I did it. If we were going to steal something, I preferred to do it myself—that way I knew the other guys wouldn't get scared and mess up.

My luck at the friendly neighborhood A&P finally ran out when I was fifteen. The door to the booth where the manager cashed checks for the customers was open one Saturday, so I went in and helped myself to the money in the cash drawer.

Somebody saw me leave and informed the manager. Of course he knew who I was and where I lived, and he notified the police. The juvenile officers picked me up at home and took me to the Youth Bureau again. By then I had hidden the money, so I kept insisting I was innocent. While I was denying everything at the Youth Bureau my brother Gerald was in our basement, playing with his dog in the coal bin where I had hidden the money. He found the money and showed it to my mother, and she called the Youth Bureau. I went back on probation.

That fall I quit school. I couldn't come home until I found a job, so I went to work in a Dairy Queen in the neighborhood. My mother sometimes stopped there after services, and I had hung around there when I was playing basketball on the church team, so the owners knew me. They even thought I was a pretty nice guy. In fact I had stolen money from them on a couple of occasions. They had little sliding windows out front, where they waited on the customers, and whenever I went by, if nobody was around, I would slide the window open, reach in, and take any money that might be in the cash drawer.

I went to work making ice cream cones and malts—and stealing. Whenever a big order came in, if the owners weren't around, I would ring up No Sale and deposit the money in my pocket. One day the owner caught me; he slapped my face and fired me. Until I began playing baseball, that was the only real job I ever had.

Six months after I was placed on probation for robbing the A&P, I was arrested again, this time for trying to crack the safe at a tobacco wholesale company. Five of us broke into the store easily enough, but the police came while we were trying to open the safe, and we all beat it out the back door. We ran into the alley and hid in someone's garage. The owner heard the commotion and came out to see what was going on. One of my friends, Louis, was so fat that the guy recognized him even in the dark. He called the police, and when the police picked up Louis he told on the rest of us.

Since I was already on probation, the judge reopened that case too, and I was sentenced to two-to-five years at the Michigan Training Unit at Ionia, Michigan. I was fifteen years old.

The Michigan Training Unit was more like a college campus than a reform school or a prison. They locked us up at night, but we had our own little rooms rather than cells. We went to school during the day. I made up my mind that as long as I had to be there, I was going to get involved in the school program and get my high school diploma. They had a little sports program at MTU, and I began thinking again about trying to win a football scholarship so I could go to college. But I blew it. I got caught stealing copies of a biology test to sell to the other kids, and I was sent across the street to finish my sentence at the Michigan Reformatory.

They had cells in the reformatory. It was just like a prison—except that most of the inmates were only seventeen or eighteen. They treated us all like little kids, never like men. I was forever breaking their silly rules to show them they couldn't treat me like that. We were supposed to walk in a certain direction whenever we came out of our cells, so I would walk in the opposite direction just to be belligerent. I did so many childish things that they threatened to transfer me to the State Prison in Jackson. They would lock me up in my cell for three or four days at a time. They wouldn't even let me out to eat; they would bring my meals to me. I suppose they were trying to show me I couldn't do whatever I wanted to do.

But I was a snotty-nosed brat who didn't give a damn about anything or anybody. When I got out of the reformatory after nineteen months my attitude was worse than ever. It wasn't that the reformatory turned me into a hardened criminal—most of the guys there didn't know as much about crime as I did—but that the officers treated us like kids. The resentment built up, and by the time I was released I hated them and all their petty rules.

Let's Shoot Some

5

Hard drugs were a big part of my life before I was old enough to get a driver's license. All the kids in the neighborhood, boys and girls, used drugs. It was the "in" thing to do. You could buy anything you wanted on the street. When I was sentenced to the Michigan Training Unit in January 1966 I was snorting heroin and cocaine regularly and shooting heroin once in a while. When I was released from the reformatory nineteen months later, I picked up where I had left off.

There was at least one dope house on every block in a seven or eight block stretch near our house. I knew where they all were, and I was able to walk right into most of them. I had visited a number of dope houses, peddling stolen clothes when I was younger, so I knew a lot of the guys who sold drugs in the neighborhood. When I began using hard drugs myself, I got pretty close to some of them. Occasionally they would let me into the private rooms where they kept their money and guns. They trusted me because I had built up a reputation for being able to steal. And I wasn't a hard-core dope addict; I still had my head together. They showed me guns—they had pistols, carbines, even machine guns. I thought, "Hey, I'm involved with people who are really criminals!" That made me feel good—real good.

They would pay me ten or fifteen dollars to let them know whenever the police were in the area, and after a while they paid me to watch the front door. They didn't like to let in anybody who wasn't using drugs—they didn't want people hanging around who were not spending money. So I let in only the guys I knew were okay, guys who used a lot of drugs. I thought I was somebody important; I figured I was really involved now.

I'm sure the police knew where all the dope houses were located as well as I did. But they probably figured they had more important crimes to solve and were trying to tighten up on the guys who were selling the drugs to the houses. Most of the guys who owned dope houses were drug addicts themselves, guys who were trying to hustle enough money to take care of their own habits.

Hanging around with them, I had the opportunity to try all kinds of drugs. Psychedelic drugs were the only kind I never tried. I liked to get high and didn't particularly care how I got there.

A few months before I was sent to the reformatory I shot heroin for the first time. A friend; Eric, and I were in a dope house where they were selling red capsules that looked like sleeping pills for a dollar apiece—Dollar Caps they called them. I bought six, three for me and three for Eric. I had already snorted drugs and I knew Eric had too, but I didn't know he had also been shooting. It surprised me when he suggested, "Let's shoot some."

I wasn't sure what I was supposed to do, so I watched Eric and did what he did. We didn't have a spoon; we used a coffee jar cover. We opened the capsules and poured the powder into the cover, then we added some water, put a match underneath, and boiled the mixture until the liquid was clear. Eric tied a handkerchief around his arm to make a tourniquet, so I did the same (though my veins were probably big enough without it).

I drew some of the liquid into the eyedropper, but I was afraid to shoot it myself. Shit, I was only fifteen. I didn't want to make a mistake—I was afraid I would get a bubble and kill myself. I asked Eric to do it for me.

He popped the needle in my arm and I started squeezing the eye dropper into the other end of the needle as slowly as I could. All of a sudden I felt woozy all over; all my muscles seemed to be relaxing at once. When I had finished putting the liquid into my arm I nodded off.

When I woke I was so high I couldn't move. I was sitting on the edge of a bed, bobbing and weaving, trying to keep my balance, and slobber was running out of my mouth. The needle was still stuck in my arm. Eric was sitting next to me on the bed. He was the same way.

I snatched the needle and threw it on the bed. I was scared. I thought I was going to die. I had heard about people dying from shooting an overdose of drugs and I thought for sure that was what was happening to me. I couldn't pull myself together. I couldn't stand up. I cried out, "Man, I'm gonna die!" The other people in the dope house were all laughing at me. "Naw," they said, "you ain't gonna die."

I started throwing up, puking all over the place. I told

myself I was never going to shoot drugs again.

Later some of my friends convinced me that the only reason I had lost control was because it had been my first time. When I eventually learned to handle it, I found that shooting drugs gave me a great feeling. I would get so high I didn't have a care in the world. Nothing could hurt me. It was like being in a dream world. I knew what was going on around me, but there was nothing I could do about it. And I didn't care; I felt so good, so relaxed.

I didn't get a nasty taste in my mouth either, the way I did when I snorted heroin. When you snort, the powder dries up the membranes in your nose and after a while they start to drain into your mouth. It's a horrible taste—nastier than anything I have ever tasted in my life. It's even worse than castor oil. That's why guys eat a lot of candy and drink a lot of pop when they're snorting dope. They're trying to get rid of that awful taste.

The feeling you get when you snort dope isn't the same feeling you get when you shoot. When you snort, it may take fifteen minutes to start working. But when you shoot, the dope goes straight into your circulatory system. It works instantly. You get much higher shooting drugs than you do snorting, and it doesn't take as much dope. But I noticed that the people who shot drugs got addicted more often than the ones who snorted. And the people who were dying from overdoses were usually the people who were shooting. People weren't dying from snorting. I didn't want to OD, so I decided I would stick to snorting even though I got that nasty drain. I did shoot drugs now and then.

I consumed all the drugs I could afford. If I had forty or fifty dollars in my pocket, I would buy forty or fifty dollars worth of dope and do it all up.

I never reached the point where I was physically addicted, but I'm sure I was what the doctors call mentally addicted. When I got caught for armed robbery I had been using hard drugs every day for nine months straight. And before that I had been using them two or three times a week. Antoine, Leroy, and I shot a little dope before we robbed Dee's Bar, and, sitting in my cell in the county jail after we got caught, I thought for sure I was going to get sick as soon as the drugs wore off. But I didn't.

Maybe it was because all the while I was using drugs I was at least eating. I would go home during the day, and my mother would fix me something good to eat; I wasn't just munching on cookies and candy like some of the other guys. I had something in my stomach for the drugs to work on and I believe that was probably the reason I didn't become addicted. I guess it was fortunate for me that I got caught when I did because there's no telling what I might have done if I had really gotten strung out on drugs.

Shortly after I was released from the reformatory an older fellow asked me if I wanted to become his partner and open a dope house. He wanted each of us to put up two thousand dollars to get started. He had been involved in another dope house but had to quit when he caught tuberculosis. I was sure he knew the business.

I didn't have two thousand dollars at the time and I wasn't sure I could steal that much right away. When I wouldn't commit myself, he asked another guy to go in with him. They opened a joint and started selling. Before long they had made enough to open another dope house, then a couple more. They became two of the biggest dope dealers on the east side, and one guy became a millionaire.

I did sell some drugs on the streets, usually to prostitutes. Most of the girls were taking speed so that they could work all night and make a lot of money. I would buy the pills wholesale for about ten cents apiece and sell them to the girls or their pimps for fifty cents or a dollar. If a girl didn't have money and her man wouldn't buy speed for her, sometimes I'd give her the pills. I got very close to a lot of the girls that way. I didn't actually have any girls working for me, but some of them gave me money. They would hold back part of their earnings, tell their man they didn't have a good day, and give that money to me. Sometimes they'd give me fifty, sixty, even a hundred dollars.

I thought about getting a few girls and going into business for myself, but I decided there were too many hassles involved. I would have had to set my girls up in different areas and meet with various pimps to make sure it was okay for my girls to work in those locations. Since I didn't have a car, I didn't think I was capable of handling that type of situation at that time.

A lot of the girls liked me, though. They assumed I was older than I was because I was running around with older guys and I always dressed real sharp. Sometimes I would go out with the girls and have little parties, and sometimes we'd have sex. They'd agree because they knew I could do them favors like getting them pills and clothes.

Some of the pimps got mad at me, but I never took any shit from them. I knew where I could get a gun if I needed one, and I had friends up and down the street. Tough friends. I wasn't particularly worried about a pimp trying to do anything to me. They would give me funny looks, but that was about it. I figured that if they couldn't handle their own women, it was their fault.

Meanwhile my taste for drugs was getting more and

more expensive. My friends and I were stealing all the time —and still we never seemed to have money in our pockets. We had become so brash we would walk into a store, shove the lady on duty out of the way, grab the money in the cash register, and run. Or one of us would keep the clerk occupied at the far end of the store while the other emptied the cash register. We didn't care if the clerk heard the bell ring; we could snatch the money and be out the door before he got there.

Sometimes we'd get one or two hundred dollars that way, but usually we'd get only fifteen or twenty. So we began pulling bigger robberies. We robbed a candy store and a couple of dry cleaners. We had a knife, but usually we didn't need it. The places we robbed were right there in the neighborhood, and most of the victims knew us. They didn't necessarily know our names or where we lived, but they had seen us around and they knew us by sight. They could have identified us, yet they never reported the robberies to the police. They were scared. We would send them notes saying, "If you tell the police on us, we'll burn your store down." That stopped them every time.

Some of the shop owners in the neighborhood bought guns to protect themselves. After a few of my friends got shot I decided I had to find some other way to get money.

I assumed that as I got older and more experienced, other types of crime would be just as easy as stealing had been when I was a kid. I never seriously considered the possibility of getting caught; I figured it was a jinx to think about it. Older guys, guys who had gotten away with a lot of crimes, had warned me, "Don't ever think about getting caught. If you do, then you will get caught." Thoughts of the police coming after me or of going to prison never seriously entered my mind. I was so lucky that I took my luck for granted.

Before we were caught for robbing Dee's Bar, I had stolen between $30,000 and $35,000, counting all the stuff I had sold.

But as you grow older and commit larger crimes, the police begin paying more attention to you. The officers are much more interested in catching an armed robber than a kid who stole a ten-cent rubber ball.

I suppose I knew, deep down inside, that what I was doing was wrong. But I didn't feel any real guilt, probably because I was getting away with it. You never think you're doing something wrong so long as you don't get caught.

They say the law of averages always gets you in the end. Supposedly you can only do so much before you get caught. I had told myself that if I ever got caught for something really serious, I was going to quit. But when I did get caught it was too late—I was on my way to prison.

The judge said I was a menace to society. That's why he sent me to the State Prison of Southern Michigan in Jackson instead of to one of the other institutions around the state. Only the worst criminals get sent to Jackson—the murderers, the rapists, the armed robbers.

It's the largest walled prison in the world: fifty-seven acres of land inside its drab red brick walls, a city in itself, a world all its own. More than four thousand men live in Jackson, and seventy-five percent of them are black.

The prison was built by inmates from the original Jackson Prison down the road. Maybe that's why it's such a miserable-looking place. It took them twelve years (from 1924 to 1935) to build that fortress. The cell blocks form some of the outer walls. Each inmate has a cell, six feet by ten feet, with a bed, a toilet, a sink, an old desk, and a locker. After they put all that in the cell there isn't much room left for the man. Even so, you have to stay in your cell all the time unless there's a yard period, you're on a work assignment, or you have a detail to be somewhere else, such as in school or the gym.

If you get caught where you're not supposed to be, it's called "skating." The officer writes you a ticket, and you have to stay locked in your cell for the weekend without yard privileges—or you might have to go to solitary confinement.

Every night at 9:30 they lock the doors to the cells—and those doors stay locked until 6:30 the next morning, no matter what. The officers walk around counting heads, then they double-lock each door. That's the worst part of the day, knowing that you're locked up and you can't get out. I had a stereo set with earphones in my cell, and just before 9:30 I would put the earphones on and turn the music up so I couldn't hear the clicking sound of the guards double-locking the doors.

They call Jackson Prison a maximum security facility, and they mean it. Virtually nobody escapes from Jackson. The prison is just about foolproof. The walls are thirty-eight feet high (at their lowest point!), and guards armed with high-power rifles are posted all around the top. The walls are twenty-five feet thick at the base—and the base extends twelve feet underground, so tunnels are out of the question.

A few guys have busted out. While I was there two inmates hid in garbage cans, beneath the garbage, and got out that way. The guards poke the garbage with pitchforks before they let it out the gate, and both guys got stabbed, one in the head and the other in the side, but they never made a sound. The state police picked them up a short while later, driving down the interstate highway in the prison garbage truck. Another inmate had a friend fly in over the back wall in a helicopter and pick him up in the yard. He got away but was caught later. Some guys run away from the prison work camps outside the walls, but there's a fifty-dollar reward for any farmer in the area who shoots a prisoner trying to escape. For fifty bucks those farmers will shoot anything.

I soon found that it's almost as difficult to get into Jackson as it is to get out. When I arrived at the reception center on April 28, 1970, the officers gave me a thorough shakedown. They showered me, they looked up my rectum, they looked through my hair, they looked everywhere to make sure I wasn't trying to bring drugs or a weapon in with me. I had accumulated some clothes during the three months I had spent in the county jail, so I sent those home and put the forty-odd dollars I had into a prison account. Inmates aren't allowed to have money—the institution issues you scrip (based on how much money you have in your account) to spend in the prison store.

Initially I was in quarantine, where new inmates are segregated for a month or two from the rest of the prison population. When I arrived the other guys in quarantine were in the yard having a little exercise period, so I didn't know how many prisoners were in quarantine. All I knew was that as far as I could see there were cells. I assumed that that was the whole prison; I didn't realize until later that it was just one cell block.

I didn't know what to expect. I didn't know whether I was going to be able to survive among all those hardened criminals. I didn't know if I was going to be killed, or raped, or what. All the time I was on the streets, all the things I had done, I was never really scared. But I was scared now. In the county jail some guys who had been in prison told me that if anybody approached me and tried to take advantage of me, the best thing to do was to grab something and hit 'em in the head. "Just show 'em you're a fighter," they advised me, "and you won't have any problems." I made up my mind I wasn't going to let anybody take advantage of me in any way.

When the other inmates came in from the yard I spotted several guys I had known around the neighborhood. "Damn," I said to myself, "when I didn't see those guys around, I thought they had gone into the army. Here they are in Jackson, just like me. I'm not going to get hassled in here; I know too many guys."

When you enter quarantine you're supposed to wear special white coveralls for three days, until you get all your shots and the doctors finish examining you to make sure you don't have any deadly disease. You're what the other inmates call a "fish." They say your number is so new that the ink is still running off. Number B-115614, that was me.

While you're wearing those white coveralls you can't leave the cell block. You can't even go out in the yard and horse around with the rest of the guys; you're supposed to stay in your cell whenever you're not being examined. One of the guys I knew from the neighborhood had some extra clothes—a pair of blue fatigue pants and a blue shirt that the regular residents wear—and he gave them to me so I could join the other guys in the yard. My second day there I went out and played basketball and had a real good time. At least I had something to occupy my mind. I felt more relaxed; I wasn't constantly thinking about all the time I had to do.

When the doctors finished with me I began taking psychiatric and IQ tests. I guess I must have done pretty well on my first tests because they offered me a job helping to test other new inmates until my quarantine period was completed. But I refused because I wanted to work in the kitchen. I noticed that guys who worked in the kitchen were allowed to stay out of their cells during the day and didn't have to lock up all the time, as the other inmates did. They also got the chance to meet the officers and find out which ones were good guys and which ones weren't. So I applied and went to work temporarily in the kitchen, feeding the other new fish.

That I had been sentenced to Jackson Prison didn't necessarily mean I had to be confined to that particular institution. There was still a chance they might send me to one of the medium-security units around the state. I behaved pretty well in quarantine, so when I went before the Classification Board I asked to be sent back to the Michigan Training Unit at Ionia so that I could finish my high school work. My request was denied, the board said, because my crime was too serious. In order to get sent to MTU, your crime had to be something small, like breaking and entering or car theft. It also helped if you were white.

I requested Cassidy Lake, a work camp outside the walls, but the board said I had too much time to serve to be sent there right away. So I asked if I could go back to the Michigan Reformatory. I knew they used inmates from Jackson to do a lot of the work inside the reformatory, and I figured it would be easy. They told me they weren't going to let me go back to the reformatory either—because I had been running with older guys and they thought I was too smart and too criminally inclined. They felt I would influence the young kids.

The Board ordered me to stay in Jackson with the older criminals, the guys they knew I could get along with and wouldn't be able to corrupt. They claimed my crime was too harsh to send me anywhere else. "You don't dictate to us what you want," the classification officer told me. "We tell you what to do. You're the one who committed the crime. We didn't ask you to come here."

I argued with them, reasoned with them, pleaded with them. "Why are you denying me the opportunity to get an education?" I asked. "I thought I was supposed to be trying to rehabilitate myself."

They wouldn't listen. "You haven't proved to us yet that you can work," the officer said. "You have to prove that before you can go to school. You will have to work on a job assignment for a year before we'll classify you to go to school."

When they classified me to go inside the walls with the general population, I was let down. It wasn't fair. I didn't want to work, I wanted to go to school. And, dammit, I wasn't going to work. I made up my mind I was going to be a rebellious prisoner.

I read all their little rules and I told myself, "Shit, I'm not going to do any of this. I'm going to do whatever I want to do." The judge had already taken my freedom; there was no way they were going to give me a bunch of chickenshit rules to abide by too. I didn't need anybody telling me what to do.

Tough as I tried to act on the outside, I was scared on the inside. I saw all those guys walking around with scowls on their faces, trying to look hard and mean, and I was sure they really were. At first I stayed pretty much to myself. Aside from the guys I met in quarantine I wouldn't talk to anybody. But a few of us got together and played basketball in the afternoon, and word got around that I was pretty good. Inmates began coming up to me and introducing themselves as the manager of the basketball team or the baseball team, or as players on the different teams. And I started feeling more at ease. Those guys weren't approaching me like hardened criminals, threatening me or asking how much time I had to do. They assumed that because I was good at basketball I could play other sports too, and they wanted to know what positions I played—things like that. I was beginning to think prison might not be such an awful place after all.

Some of the guys invited me to practice with one of the intramural softball teams, and even though I had never played very much as a kid, I hit the hell out of the ball. The next day the manager of the varsity softball team asked me if I'd like to try out. I had heard that if you got on a varsity team, you had it made because the varsity players were privileged people in the institution. They didn't have to lock up in their cells during the day and they could hang around the gym when they weren't working. So I jumped at the invitation.

I wasn't eligible to join a varsity team until I had been classified for a work assignment, so I reported to the Classification Board and asked to be assigned to the kitchen again. Instead I was classified to work in the tailored garment factory, where they made fatigues for the prisoners and uniforms for the officers not only in Jackson but in all the institutions around the state.

On my first day I was assigned to the "bag line," where we made the huge heavy canvas bags that the inmates threw their dirty sheets and linen into. I had never used a sewing machine in my life, but they put me right to work on a heavy-duty machine with a fat needle. It was the worst job in the place.

I couldn't keep up with production. The civilian supervisor showed me how to do it a couple of times, but I still couldn't keep up, and on the second day he began screaming at me.

"Look, man," I shouted back, "I haven't done this work before and I can't do it!"

"What do you mean you can't do it?" he hollered.

"I just can't," I said. I kicked my sewing machine and I walked away.

He fired me and turned in a report, but it was almost four months before the report was processed and I was called back to classification. Meanwhile I was allowed to play softball all summer. We practiced every afternoon and played on the weekend. I couldn't believe prison could be so much fun.

I Ain't No Farmer

7

They let me out of Jackson in September. I was transferred outside the walls to the Dalton Farm, where they raised pigs, cows, and chickens and grew crops to feed the inmates. I had heard about the farm where you slept in barracks instead of a cell block and were free to walk around. You could even walk away at night if you wanted to. It sounded like a good job.

On all the details they expected the inmates to start at the bottom and work their way through the system, so I was assigned to a crew known as the "piss hats." They had to do all the dirty jobs on the farm, like shoveling cow shit, chicken shit, and pig shit. At harvest time they had to pick potatoes.

Since it was September when I got there, the potatoes were ready to be picked. In the morning they ran a potato digger through the patch and the potatoes literally jumped out of the ground by the thousands. The "piss hats" had to pick them all up and put them in crates. When I got back to the barracks after my first day in the field, I was covered with black muck from the potato patch. I couldn't get clean, even in the shower, and then and there I decided I wasn't doing that job anymore. It wasn't only dirty work, it was bad on your back. All day you waded through muck, bent over, picking up potatoes.

The next morning I ate breakfast with the rest of the guys, but when we got to the field I informed the man in charge, "You might as well write me a ticket because I can't do this work.

"It's too hard," I told him. "Besides, I ain't no farmer. I'm not gonna pick potatoes when I leave here, so why should I pick potatoes now? I'm just gonna sit here on the truck all day."

I sat there too, smoking cigarettes and watching the other guys pick potatoes. Harvey, the civilian in charge of the crew, walked by several times and said, "You'd better get your ass out there and pick those potatoes."

I just sneered at him. "You're a bunch of shit, man," I said. "Fuck you!"

When we returned to the barracks after work he wrote up a ticket on me and sent it to the prison. About 5:30, while we were eating dinner, a guard came and told me to pick up my clothes because I was going back inside the walls. I went straight to solitary confinement.

I knew what was coming when I refused to work. It was automatic; anytime you refused to do a job you got indefinite solitary confinement. But I preferred solitary to picking those potatoes.

The cells in solitary were the same size as those in the general population, but all that was in them was a toilet, a sink, and a cot that was bolted to the floor. There was no mattress. You got two blankets, no sheets, and you had to make a pad of one of the blankets so your body wouldn't be up against the metal cot.

When you were sent to solitary they took away all your clothes and gave you a pair of white coveralls and a pair of grey socks. No shoes, no underwear, no pajamas. They gave you a little toilet paper to wipe your ass, but you weren't allowed to have soap in your cell. You got to shower and shave once a week, but you couldn't brush your teeth unless you got a visitor. And when you were in solitary you were only permitted two visits a month.

Other than that, you never saw anybody except the hall boys who brought your food. You weren't allowed to smoke, although the hall boys would occasionally slip you a cigarette. You weren't supposed to talk either, but if you were careful, you could talk quietly with the guy in the cell next to you. You almost had to whisper, and you had to keep peeking down the hall, watching for the officer, because if you got caught talking in solitary, they automatically threw you in the slammer for seven days. That meant seven days when you couldn't see anything and couldn't hear anything because there was a heavy steel door instead of bars in front of your cell. You really had to be careful.

There was no reading in solitary either. All you could do was sit, hour after hour, playing with your lower lip. At mealtime you got half as much food as the other inmates, and you were allowed only two meals a day instead of three. For dinner you might get a meat pattie about the size of a small hamburger, a little scoop of potatoes, a scoop of mixed vegetables, and a slice of bread. That was it. And you didn't get any yard privileges at all.

After I had been living like that for two weeks they brought me out of solitary.

"Do you want to go back and work on the farm now?" the officer asked.

"No!" I said, shaking my head. "No way in the world will I go back there and do that dirty job!"

"Then we'll see you in another month," the officer said.

I was really mad then. I cussed the guards out, calling them all kinds of sons of bitches as they took me back to my cell in solitary. After I had calmed down I began thinking about different things I might do to pass the time. It was getting terribly boring in there.

It's so quiet in solitary it gnaws on your nerves after a while. I actually heard guys go crazy. Someone would start screaming, and the next thing you knew the officers would be taking the guy to the psychiatric ward. When he came back—if he came back—he'd be as batty as could be. I thought to myself, "Man, I gotta do something or I'm gonna go crazy too."

I began doing jumping jacks in my cell, and I noticed that it not only helped me stay warm on chilly days, it also tired me out so I could fall asleep. So I started doing sit-ups and push-ups too. I wasn't in very good shape; I couldn't do many at first. After about ten I would be out of breath. I kept at it and before long I was able to do twenty-five sit-ups and twenty-five push-ups. I gradually built myself up until I was able to do two sets of twenty-five each, every day. Then I started doing three sets a day, then four. I increased to fifty sit-ups and fifty push-ups in each set, and finally, after about three weeks, I was able to do one hundred sit-ups and one hundred push-ups at a time. I would do one hundred of each in the morning and one hundred of each at night.

I noticed that my chest had expanded and my arms were getting stronger. I always had strong legs, so I began doing little bicycle exercises to keep them in shape. I walked a lot, too. I could take three steps, turn around, take three steps in the opposite direction, and turn again. I walked like that for two or three hours every day just to pass the time. Three steps, turn around; three steps, turn around. I did so much walking it was pathetic.

When my month was up they hauled me out again. "You ready to go to the farm now?"

Again I replied, as defiantly as ever, "Nope."

"Okay," the officer said, "you're going to find out you don't run this place, we run it. We'll see you in another month."

After a couple of weeks they relented a little and moved me upstairs to another detention area where at least I was allowed to read and have some cigarettes. They even let me brush my teeth.

My mother came to visit me twice while I was in solitary, and I told her to ask the officials if I could go to school and get my high school diploma. She made a special trip to Jackson to see them. A prison official assured my mother I would be permitted to go to school, but I never budged from solitary.

I was allowed to write letters after I had been transferred upstairs, so I wrote to Gus Harrison, then the head of the State Department of Corrections, requesting my release from solitary confinement. I stated I felt I was being treated unfairly.

I kept waiting for a response, but it never came. When Harrison visited the prison on an inspection tour, I called to him from my cell and asked if he had received my letter.

"I haven't received anything from you," he replied.

"Well, I wrote you," I explained, "saying I felt I was being treated unfairly here, but I guess the officer who censored my mail never sent it to you."

Harrison must have mentioned it to one of the guards because after he left a group of officers came to my cell. I could see they were pissed off. "We sent your letter out," one of them snarled. "He didn't respond because he didn't think you had the right to write to him and complain about how this institution is being run."

Then they opened my cell door and charged me—all five or six of them. It was a real goon squad. I fought back, but I knew there was no way I could win, so I just tried to protect myself. I knew that if I didn't, they would really mess over me. I tucked my head into one guard's chest so they couldn't get at my face, and I started swinging away.

After they had beat me up they took me downstairs and threw me in the slammer for fighting. I was furious. I hurt like hell all over, and there wasn't a damn thing I could do about it. When you're in the slammer you can't send correspondence out and you can't have visitors.

There are no beds in the slammer—you sleep on the floor. They give you two blankets and your coveralls, and that's it. If you're really bad, they take your coveralls away. The cells in the slammer are only about half the size of the regular cells, and they're solid on all four sides. Unless a guard opens the shutter on the peep hole in the steel door, no light gets in at all. It's pitch black. You have to feel your way around even when you go to the toilet.

When the tours come through the prison—congressmen, reporters, and people like that—the guards don't let them near the detention area where the slammers are located. I'm sure some of the conditions there are unconstitutional. Unless you've been in there there's no way you can know what it's really like. It's that horrible.

Finally, after a total of three and a half months in solitary and in the slammer, they let me out. They didn't ask me if I was willing to go back to the Dalton Farm—I guess they realized I wasn't going to pick anybody's potatoes. They simply told me I had been classified to work in the shoe factory.

I didn't want that job either, but I was sick of being cooped up, so I didn't say a word. I told myself, "I'll be damned if I'll live by their rules." I hadn't been out for a month when I was caught with some spud juice (the moonshine alcohol that many of the inmates drink), and I was sent back to solitary.

I was hardheaded, no doubt about that. When I went to prison I assumed I was going to continue to be involved in crime when I got out. I planned to meet people with good drug connections and to open up a dope house. I also thought about pulling some more robberies, and I made it a point to introduce myself to inmates who had reputations for being good burglars and good armed robbers, and I tried to learn all I could from them. They told me about the places they had robbed and the money they had taken. I would sit in my cell at night, trying to think of places I could rob when I got out of prison.

I recalled a Brinks armored truck that came to the neighborhood A&P every Saturday morning at about ten o'clock and invariably got caught at the stoplight on the corner of Van Dyke and Mack. I devised a plan to rob that armored truck. I knew there was a sewer in the street, near the corner, and I decided I would get dynamite and hide in the sewer. When the Brinks truck stopped for the light I would come out of the sewer, shove the dynamite under the truck, and light a match to it. I figured I would have friends waiting down the street to help gather up the money when the truck blew up.

I had seen crooks snatch army payrolls in the movies, and I was thinking about trying that too. I figured it would be a good way to get a lot of money at once. I had also heard inmates talking about robbing a Federal Reserve shipment, and I thought about trying that. I was planning to get even with Leroy for squealing on me, too.

When I went to solitary confinement for the second time I put all those ideas out of my head. I wouldn't say I was thinking about going straight and becoming an upstanding citizen when I got out, but I realized that if I didn't change my ways, I was never going to get out of that institution.

Sitting in my cell in solitary, I thought, "You fool, you dumb fucking fool! You're not doing yourself any good—all you're doing is keeping the prison people in jobs. You can't tear this place down by yourself!"

I decided that as long as I had to be in prison I was going to take whatever job they gave me when I got out of solitary. "Here it is 1971," I thought. "I've been here for about a year and I've got two more years until I go before the parole board. The way I'm going that'll be a waste of time because there's no way they'll let me out. And I've got to get out of here."

I kept doing my exercises in solitary, getting myself into top shape so that when I was allowed to rejoin the general population I would be ready to take part in sports and to build the sort of reputation that would eventually get me released from prison.

They kept me in solitary for two and a half months the second time, then they classified me to work in the textile factory, where they made the sheets and pillow cases for all the penal institutions in the state. I was back where I had started, on sewing machines—but these machines were much smaller than those in the tailored garment factory, and I was able to operate them.

After a couple of days I was fired again—not for refusing to work, but for talking too much. I had been in solitary for so long that when I got out and could finally talk again without being hassled by the officers, I didn't want to stop.

Since I hadn't refused to work, they didn't throw me back into solitary. The day after I was fired I happened to see out in the yard one of the guys I had worked with in the quarantine kitchen. I told him to ask the kitchen steward to put in a formal request for me, and finally I was classified to work in the kitchen. The Classification Board told me I couldn't change jobs again for at least six months, no matter what. I had to have a good work report and I couldn't go on sick call.

I didn't mind. I knew I could handle the work in the kitchen because it wasn't that hard. I also knew I was going to be able to do whatever I wanted to do on the side.

Wheeling and Dealing

If a guy wanted to be wheeling and dealing while he was in prison, the kitchen was the best place to be. There were all sorts of ways you could make extra money working in the kitchen; before long I had tried them all.

They put me right to work on the morning cook gang, which was responsible for breakfast and lunch. When I wasn't unloading the big pots as they came back from the dishwasher, I was leaning over the hot grill, frying pancakes, french toast, and eggs. When bacon and eggs were on the menu we had to get up at three o'clock in the morning to fry the eggs and have them ready when the residents broke for breakfast at 6:30. Each guy on the grill got ten crates of eggs to fry.

I had cooked a little bit at home when I was growing up, but that was nothing compared to cooking for six thousand men. When I was four years old my mother was very sick for awhile, and I cooked dinner for the family. I made black-eyed peas, corn bread, neck bones—everything. Mother couldn't get out of bed, so I took the ingredients to her bedroom and she told me what to do. When my father came home from work he couldn't believe it. When I was six I loved to bake cookies. Mother bought me one of those cookie makers that you screw to make the cookies come out in different shapes. I would come home from school, get out the ingredients, and make cookies. Now, instead of little pinches of things, I was using ingredients by the pound.

I did so well in the kitchen that when the second cook was promoted (after I had been there about a month) they gave me his job. The second cook was responsible for preparing the gravies and cooking the vegetables, and I had to learn to make gravy in eighty-gallon vats. I would take fifty pounds of lard, melt it down, add one hundred fifty or two hundred pounds of flour, and whip it with a big paddle to make the roux. The grease would be a foot deep in the vat, and the flour would weigh about five hundred pounds when it had been wet down, but I'd whip it for thirty minutes to get it smooth. Then I would add the broth. In no time at all I got to be a pretty good cook—if I do say so myself.

As second cook I was also responsible for taking inventory and ordering the food for the kitchen. That was the part of the job I enjoyed. I would go to the commissary and get the supplies we needed in the kitchen—and anything else I wanted for myself.

As soon as I became second cook I began selling tomato puree, yeast, and the other ingredients for making the illegal home brew called spud juice that was so popular in the prison. Since we weren't allowed to have money inside the walls, we dealt in cigarettes. The more cigarettes an inmate had, the more he was worth. I charged five packs of cigarettes for a gallon of puree. You could make a hundred gallons of spud juice with a pound of yeast, so I would cut a pound into ten pieces and charge a carton of cigarettes per chunk. I sold sugar for a pack of cigarettes a pound. I let the inmates in the commissary know what I wanted, and they hid it on my cart with the regular order.

My customers would come to the kitchen to pick up the ingredients they had ordered. There were usually a few officers around, but they couldn't watch everybody. The best time to make a delivery was during meal time, when all the officers were on the serving line, watching the other inmates and trying to keep the commotion down. I'd go around later in the day to collect my cigarettes and split them with my partners in the commissary.

When I found out how much money there was to be made, I began making spud juice and selling it myself. Five packs of cigarettes was the going price for a six-ounce jar of spud juice. I would take an empty plastic jug, put in a pound and a half of sugar and a cup of tomato puree, add water, shake it all up, and then add the yeast. I'd put the cover on loosely so the stuff wouldn't explode, and I'd hide it.

At first the ingredients floated on top while they were fermenting. Then, when the spud juice was ready, everything would fall to the bottom. If you let it set too long, the spud juice would turn to vinegar.

Where you hid the stuff while it was fermenting depended on how much guts you had. A lot of guys hid it in their cells, even though the stuff stunk after a couple of days and there was always the chance a guard would smell it. I hid spud juice in my cell a couple of times, but usually I left it in the kitchen where it was nice and warm. Better yet I would get another inmate to hide it in his cell for me; that way I wouldn't run the risk of being caught and sent to solitary. Some guys would go for that too because I'd give them four cartons of cigarettes for hiding the stuff—plus enough spud juice to get drunk on.

I don't know what the alcohol content was, but it was potent enough to get a person bombed. It tasted sort of like a bloody mary—without lime and Tabasco, of course.

You could always tell when someone had spud juice for sale. You would see guys coming out of the different cell blocks carrying cartons of cigarettes under their arms, and a short while later you'd see the same guys running back to their cells carrying little brown bags. News travels fast in the institution; everybody knows when something is going on.

I'm sure the officers knew what was happening, too. All they had to do was look at all the guys running around carrying cigarettes. And there were informers all over the institution. But the guards didn't have the manpower to stop everyone, so they would see it—but they wouldn't see it. They could catch you anytime they wanted to, and some guys always seemed to get caught while others never did. Usually the guys who got caught were those who were causing the guards a lot of problems.

With cigarettes you could buy anything you wanted: spud juice, food, heroin, cocaine, grass, acid, speed—even real money. Four cartons of cigarettes were worth a ten-dollar bill.

A lot of inmates had real money even though it was against the rules and you could only spend scrip in the prison store. Some guys carried two or three thousand dollars around with them at times. The majority of the cash money in the institution belonged to white guys who were supposedly in the Mafia. Black inmates who had a lot of money usually had been big dope dealers on the street. Some of them had things set up for themselves in prison the same way. They were the kingpins, and they had their lieutenants (or whatever you want to call them) distributing drugs for them within the prison. If anyone got caught, it was always the little guy.

I don't know how the dope got into the institution, but there was no way the inmates could have brought it in—or the knives and guns that were found there either. Security was too tight. Officers must have smuggled the stuff in and sold it to the inmates. I'm not saying I can name officers who did that, but I will say, without question, that there were officers who brought money into the institution—and probably drugs too. Corruption was everywhere. I'll bet an inmate could get a woman in there, if he slipped an officer enough money.

Working in the kitchen, I was selling everything I could get my hands on. I was always up to something, but I walked around as innocent as could be. A friend, Ponderosa, called me The Cobra because no one knew where I would strike next.

Most of my crimes were petty compared to what I had been doing on the street. I would do things just to get away with something, to pass the time. A friend who worked on the crew that peeled potatoes would steal lettuce, I would steal salad oil, lunch meat, and cheese, and we would make big salads to eat in gym. The officer on duty in the gym was a big, fat guy who was always hungry. As long as we gave him something to eat, he looked the other way.

I also liked to go to the movies. We were only allowed to go once a week, but I would bribe the inmate on the desk with a couple packs of cigarettes, and he would let me in every day. I'd steal corned beef from the kitchen for sandwiches, buy potato chips and pop, sneak it all into the movie, and have a picnic. Little things like that meant a lot.

Most of the guards and administrators didn't care for me because they heard I was doing all those things and they couldn't catch me. Officers would stop me in the yard and say, "You're con-wise—you're getting away with too much. But we're going to get you."

As I accumulated more and more cigarettes, I began establishing myself in other businesses. If a guy wanted to buy drugs but didn't have enough cigarettes, I would buy his watch from him for, say, ten cartons. Later I would sell his watch back to him for fifteen cartons of cigarettes. That way he got his drugs and, eventually, he got his watch back, too. Before long I had so many cartons of cigarettes that I was considered a rich inmate. I usually could lay my hands on a hundred cartons, given an hour's notice. An inmate was allowed to keep only ten cartons in his cell, so I had guys all around holding cigarettes for me.

I had quite a bit of real money, too; I made between four and five thousand dollars while I was in prison. I would loan money two for one: If I loaned an inmate one hundred dollars, I got two hundred back. I may have decided to straighten myself out, but I hadn't turned stupid. Some guys would borrow money and neglect to pay it back—and that always caused a little confusion. I would have to pressure them a bit. Sometimes a guy would ask to be locked up for his own protection. When that happened I was usually out the money. Fortunately it didn't happen very often.

Once a guy who owed me money had himself locked up and I bribed another inmate to drop a threatening note in his cell. The guy turned the note in to the officers, and they thought it wasn't safe to let him back into the general population, so they sent him to Dalton Farm. But the fool escaped. When they caught him they put him back inside the walls again. And I was able to get my money back.

As you might imagine, there was a lot of homosexuality in the prison. It was dangerous to mess with another guy's homosexual—that was the number one reason why inmates were beaten up and killed.

The guards tried to keep homosexuals in a cell block away from the other inmates, but there were too many of them. There were a lot of undercover homosexuals, too, that the officers didn't know about. Whenever a new inmate arrived the homosexuals would try to find out how strong he was. If they found a weak guy, they'd give him cigarettes and candy; then one day they would tell the guy he owed them. That was one way homosexuals approached a new man about having sex with them.

Another way was to have friends beat up the new guy. While his friends were messing with the guy the homosexual would appear and say, "Hey, leave that guy alone." The new guy would naturally think the homosexual was his friend. A lot of inmates were recruited into homosexuality that way. It didn't necessarily mean they were going to be homosexuals for the rest of their lives; it was just their way of surviving while they were in the institution.

Some homosexuals even arranged to have their boy friends moved into the cell next to them. While everybody else was going to breakfast the bully would go into the cell where his lover stayed and do whatever he wanted to do with the kid.

Most of the homosexual activity went on in the yard. Guys would have sex under the bleachers on the baseball field, where the guards in the towers couldn't see them. A lot of guys got crapped on doing that—literally. One would be pumping the other in the butt and it would get messy as hell. I saw a lot of guys come running from behind the bleachers with crap on the front of their clothes, trying to get back to their cells to change before an officer caught them. It was horrible.

I was approached by a homosexual only once, when I first got out of quarantine. I made up my mind I wasn't going to let anybody take advantage of me, so when a guy came to my cell and suggested we get together, I agreed to meet him by the gym. When I got there I was looking around, trying to act cool, until I spotted a baseball bat leaning against the building. I grabbed the bat and whacked the homosexual in the head. Down he went.

"Hey, man," he sobbed, holding his hands in front of his face, "I didn't mean no harm. I was just seeing what kind of guy you were." I hit him a couple more times, then I dropped the bat and began kicking him.

"I'm a man!" I shouted. "I ain't no homosexual!" I never was approached again. Word gets around.

I met a lot of guys who were homosexuals or who were involved with homosexuals while they were in prison, and some of them were really nice people. We became friends. But I could never bring myself to do anything like that.

It was hard being in prison and not being able to have a woman. It was real hard. But I could never bring myself to the point where I could poke a homosexual in the butt. Sometimes I would sit in my cell and think about a woman and masturbate. I did my share in the three and a half years I was in prison.

I did get caught in one situation that involved a homosexual. I had a bad acne problem when I first went to prison, and one day a homosexual suggested I put some Noxzema on my face. I had never been concerned much about my appearance (I thought only women used makeup), but I told him to get me some Noxzema. The homosexual's boy friend saw us talking, and I guess he figured I was trying to steal his lover. He beat him up and told him he was going to kill me. My homosexual friend warned me about it, and I told some friends. While we were talking we spotted a friend of the guy who had threatened me spying on us, and we chased him into the sanitation department and whacked him. When that happened the guy who had said he was going to kill me went to the officers and claimed I was trying to kill him. I guess he figured he was next. My intention was only to protect myself—but he locked himself up. He had gotten so involved with the homosexual that the situation affected his mind, and he was sent to the psychiatric ward.

There were a lot of nuts walking around in prison who didn't belong there. You never knew when one of them was going to jump you. While a guy in my block was sleeping one night, the inmate in the next cell poured flammable glue from the shoe factory over his head and set him on fire. By the time the officers got to him he was burned so badly the skin was rolling off him. I heard later he had slapped the other guy's lover. The fellow who had burned him was already doing life for murder, so he simply got another life sentence added on. A lot of us didn't sleep too soundly for a long while after that—we all knew we might be next.

Twinkle Toes Bosco

9

Sports were merely another con, another hustle for me.
I became involved in athletics because the guys who played
sports stood a better chance of getting an early parole (if
they kept their noses clean). When you played sports you got
to meet the right people, the prison officials and others who
might be able to help you out. You were also able to build
a rapport with the officers so you wouldn't get hassled so
much. And it was a good way to pass the time.

At first I only played softball, but there was a homosexual on the squad—the son of a bitch was always grabbing
guys by the pants, trying to feel them up—and in the spring
of 1971 I got disgusted and quit.

I tried out for baseball even though I had never hit a
hard ball with a real baseball bat in my life, and I made the
team. On May 18, 1971, I believe, I played in my first real
baseball game.

We had quite a team. The catcher was doing ten-to-twenty for armed robbery; the first baseman was doing twenty-to-forty for armed robbery; the second baseman and shortstop were both doing life for murder; the third baseman was serving seven-and-a-half-to-fifteen for robbery; I was in left field; the centerfielder was doing seven-and-a-half-to-fifteen for manslaughter; the rightfielder was doing twenty-to-forty for rape; and our pitcher was serving ten-to-twenty for rape.

I played baseball with those guys every day, and I kept improving and improving. We practiced each afternoon and on the weekend played games against semi-pro and amateur teams from around the state. Our schedule consisted entirely of home games. (The prison officials frowned on road trips.)

Guys on the visiting teams commented on how good I was, and some of the managers asked where I had learned to play baseball. When I told them I had started playing in prison, they couldn't believe it.

I could hit the ball a long way and I could run. Other than that, I didn't know what I was doing. Nobody taught me how to slide or how to catch a fly ball. I would take off running and slide into the base any way I could. Sometimes I'd go straight in on my butt, sometimes I'd dive at the bag —anything to get there. We didn't have signs or signals or anything as sophisticated as that. I didn't even know such things existed.

When I began playing baseball I met Jimmy Karalla, an older guy, about forty or so, who was good at athletics and knew a lot about sports. He was doing four-to-twenty for extortion and was said to be tough, but that didn't bother me.

We both hung around the gym so much that we got to

be good friends. We talked sports all the time. Karalla told me he thought I had professional baseball potential. I knew I was a good athlete, but I had never thought about baseball as anything more than a way to impress the administration and pass the time.

Karalla kept working with me. He hit me grounders and fly balls and taught me how to slide. He clocked me on the football field: 9.6 seconds for one hundred yards where the grass was six inches high and the ground wasn't level. He kept telling me I had the ability to play professional baseball. The more he talked about it, the more I thought about it. I began believing that maybe I could play professional ball when I got out of prison, so I began watching games on TV, trying to learn as much as possible. In August 1971 I wrote to the Detroit Tigers, to General Manager Jim Campbell, requesting a tryout after I was released. The Tigers sent me a form letter in September, stating that all their players were scouted and they weren't interested.

I continued to play baseball nonetheless. I put on a lot of weight in prison—I was up around two hundred thirty pounds—and friends began calling me Bosco because I was fat and easygoing like Bosco Bear in the chocolate drink commercials. Guys on the baseball team called me Twinkle Toes because I could run so fast. Eventually people put the two names together and I was Twinkle Toes Bosco.

The prison newspaper, *The Spectator*, picked up the nickname and began using it in the headlines. One week the paper would say, "Twinkle Toes Bosco Stars at Plate, 6-for-6." The next week the headline would be "Twinkle Toes Bosco Homers Again." My name was in the headlines all the time. I hit .469 in 1971, my first year playing baseball. I hit .569 the next year.

*Ron LeFlore's athletic exploits did not go
entirely unnoticed by teams that visited the
penitentiary to play the inmates. Les Davis, the
manager of a semi-pro team from Muskegon,
Michigan, and a part-time scout for the Milwaukee
Brewers, thought enough of Ron's ability to write a
letter to his big league superiors in 1972, suggesting
they scout him further. He was told not to bother;
the Milwaukee Brewers weren't interested.*

I played all sports and played them well. I was the best
baseball player in the institution at the time, I was the best
football player, and while I wasn't the best basketball player
I was one of the best. I developed a reputation as the best
athlete ever to go through that institution—and there have
been some good athletes in Jackson.

In my first year of football I was named captain of the
team. We had just begun using the wishbone offense in 1971
and I played left halfback; I was also the punter, the kickoff
return man, the punt return man, and occasionally the
flanker. Whenever we couldn't move the ball on the ground
I'd tell the quarterback, "Throw the ball in the air as far as
you can, and I'll run under it." I threw the halfback option
pass, too, but no one on the team could catch the ball. I also
played a little defense. I was a real workhorse.

We played good football in the institution, mostly
against small college teams from the area. We would scrimmage against guys who hadn't played much the previous
week in the regular game. In a game against Hillsdale College I received the opening kickoff and ran the ball back
about forty yards, then ran about twenty-five yards more on
a sweep around the right end. When we got down to the

twelve-yard line the quarterback gave me another pitch and I went in for the touchdown.

Muddy Waters, the coach of the Hillsdale team, was so impressed he sent one of his assistants to find out my name. The assistant coach said Waters was considering offering me a scholarship to Hillsboro when I was released. Muddy Waters sent me a letter stating he was going to see if he could get me a special parole. I wrote back to tell him I'd like to go to college and play football and, if he was really interested, would he please send me some equipment so I could work out? The equipment we had in prison had been salvaged from various colleges and was badly beaten up.

Waters sent me shoes, shoulder pads, and a helmet, and I went around the prison telling everyone I was going to play college football.

The following year, 1972, the institution canceled our football schedule. They claimed they didn't have enough money in the budget. I never heard from Muddy Waters again.

The assistant athletic director, Kermit Smith, had played football under Duffy Daugherty at Michigan State University, and he told Duffy what a good football player I was. Duffy said that if he got the head coaching job with the Buffalo Bills in the National Football League, he would give me a tryout. Unfortunately he didn't get the job. (Imagine O. J. Simpson and me in the same backfield!)

Four or five times a month my mother would come to Jackson to visit me. If it happened to be a Sunday, my father and my brother Gerald would come too. My parents didn't have a car, so they either asked a friend to drive them or caught the Greyhound bus. During the week my mother would catch the bus to Jackson at seven o'clock in the morning, then take the noon bus back to Detroit and go straight to Howard Johnson's, where she worked until midnight.

My mother is not a very strong woman, physically, and I often wondered where she got the strength to do all the things she did. I mean, she was always working so the family could make ends meet, and she still found time to take care of the house and us kids, too. I don't know how she did it.

My mother has had a lot of sorrow in her life, too. After my brother Harold died, she got sick and didn't do anything but sit around the house for almost a whole year. She wouldn't go out of the house, except to the doctor's office. It was really hard on her.

Then, to see me go to prison . . . I still don't know how she withstood it.

I didn't want her to suffer any more than she already had, and I knew all those trips to Jackson had to be hard on her, with her working and all, so I told her one visit a month would be sufficient. I really didn't care to have a lot of visits anyway, and I couldn't see any sense in putting her through all that trouble for nothing. My mother couldn't understand that—she would have come to visit me every day if she could have—but that was the way I felt.

Few people knew where I was. My mother was too ashamed to tell most of the people in the neighborhood, and I didn't see any reason to notify my friends. I didn't even tell my girl friend, Deborah Hutchins. She thought I was in the army. I wrote her a few times without putting a return address on the letter. (I figured she wouldn't look at the postmark.) I told her not to bother writing because I was moving around so much in the service that her letter probably wouldn't reach me anyway. I told her to do whatever she wanted to as far as getting together with other guys in the

I guess I was destined to be a ballplayer, but I can't say I did it the easy way. (*The LeFlore Collection*)

You keep your number for life.
(*Southern Michigan State Prison*)

I got out of prison on July 2, 1973, and three days later I was wearing another uniform, representing the Tigers' farm team, the Clinton (Iowa) Pilots, in the Midwest League. (*Detroit Tigers*)

That's the trophy I won as Most Valuable Player in the Florida State League in 1974, when I played for the Lakeland Tigers. *(Detroit Tigers)*

On my first day with the Tigers, August 1, 1974, manager Ralph Houk stunned me when he said, "You're starting tonight. You're going to be my centerfielder and you're going to lead off." *(UPI)*

This is the supermarket I robbed more than once as a kid. Through that window I was able to reach into the cash drawer—and when I got caught I was placed on probation. (*Dan Dmitruck*)

I lived in this house for eight years (1958–1965). When I sneaked out at night, I would jump off the porch roof. (*Dan Dmitruck*)

I'm visiting my old neighborhood "playground." It still doesn't have any AstroTurf. *(Dan Dmitruck)*

This is not one of my 23 stolen bases in 1974. Umpire Russ Goetz has just called me out on a tag by Doug Griffin of the Red Sox. *(UPI)*

Would you believe a tomato plant in front of the centerfield fence at Tiger Stadium? As centerfielder, I'm taking care of it. *(UPI)*

Me and The Bird. There's nothing phony about Mark Fidrych, he truly is crazy. He's a great guy. I love him! *(Dan Dmitruck)*

I'm tripling here against Baltimore to extend my hitting streak to 30 games in 1976, but the Yankees' Ed Figueroa and Tippy Martinez ended it in the next game. *(UPI)*

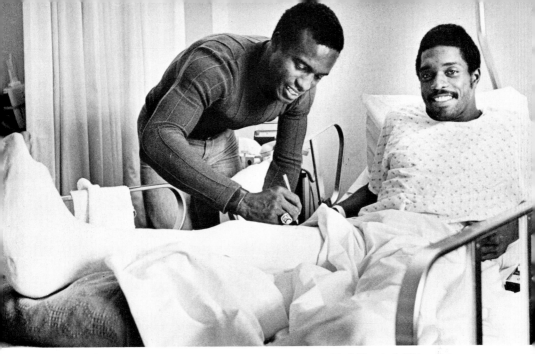

My teammate, Ben Oglivie, is signing my cast in Henry Ford Hospital. This was in September 1976, after I ruptured a tendon in my right knee. (*Bob Scott −Detroit* Free Press)

Who would have thought people would be lining up one day to get my autograph?
(*Bob Scott −Detroit* Free Press)

I'm at home with Deborah and our daughter LaRonda. *(Dan Dmitruck)*

neighborhood; I didn't want her making promises she wasn't going to keep.

I didn't know what I was going to do when I got out, but I made up my mind I wasn't ever coming back to prison. In the institution you get a number, and you keep that number for life in case you're sent back to prison. I saw so many guys with numbers that dated back to the 1940s and early 1950s that it opened my eyes. What kind of life can that be? I asked myself. Guys would leave on parole one week and be back the next week. I certainly didn't want to be running in and out of prison for the rest of my life.

Most of the guys I hung around with in prison were older than I was, just as it was on the street—but for a different reason. In prison the older guys were more settled while the younger guys were more daring, always stirring up trouble, getting into fights, talking about trying to escape. The older guys didn't want to show off; they just wanted to do their time and get out. That was the way I felt, too.

I met one old guy, Rabbit Spencer, who had been in and out of the institution for twenty-five years. He had been using drugs that long, too. For some reason he seemed to pay close attention to me. Whenever he saw me doing something wrong, like "skating" into another cell block, he would call me aside and say, "Look, man, you shouldn't be doing that.

"It don't make sense for you to ruin your life when you've got a chance to make something of yourself," he told me. "I've been in and out of this place, and the way you're going, you're going to be doing the same thing. I've been through it, man, and there ain't no glory here. You've got too much going for you to spend the rest of your life in institutions. You're the best athlete I've ever seen come through here—you're stronger, you're faster, and from what I've seen your thinking is a little better, too.

"Don't blow it, man. It's much easier to blow an opportunity than it is to get one."

I guess he caught me at the right time, when I already had intentions of trying to change myself for the better. A lot of guys tried to offer me advice, and I listened to them —but I wouldn't hear them. It was different with Rabbit Spencer because I knew he had done all the things I was thinking about doing. It was easier to pay attention to him because he knew what he was talking about. He probably wanted to better himself, too, but it was too late.

I lay in my cell at night after the lights were out, thinking about the things he said and wondering, Was he right? Rabbit Spencer had a lot of influence on me and on my decision to change my life.

There were others too. Reggie Harding, who attended Eastern High School in Detroit and later played for the Detroit Pistons in the National Basketball Association, was in Jackson for a while. Occasionally we played basketball together. Just before he was released he told me the Baltimore Bullets were giving him a chance to get back into pro basketball.

"You gonna go straight?" I asked him.

He glared at me as if I had no business asking him a question like that. "Whattaya mean, am I gonna go straight?" he sneered.

Soon after he got out word came back to the prison that he was using drugs again. A short time later I heard he had been shot and killed. That made me stop and think.

After I had put in my mandatory six months working in the kitchen I was allowed to go to school half a day. I had been in the tenth grade when I quit high school, and in prison I got my diploma. I took the high school equivalency test just to be sure.

I quit using hard drugs not because I had to—there were plenty of drugs around—but because I didn't want the hassles drugs caused. I did get some dope a couple of times. I heard so much about psychedelic drugs that I even tried some mescaline one night, but I wasn't looking to buy drugs all the time the way some inmates were. I would toke on a little grass now and then just to break the monotony, but that was about it. I first got involved in drugs in high school because I was curious—now I didn't feel that need anymore. I even joined Narcotics Anonymous because I knew it would look good on my record when I came up for parole. In fact I got involved in as many different programs as I could. I participated in group counseling and Alcoholics Anonymous, and I even started going to church regularly, just to get those things on my record. I wanted to convince the parole board that I had been rehabilitated and deserved to be released.

And I really had changed. A lot of people noticed it. I noticed the change too, and I began patting myself on the back because I could see the improvement myself.

My best friend in the institution, Shorty George Grimmett, and I set up an athletic program for the inmates in the psychiatric ward. They were mostly disturbed kids, sixteen or seventeen years old, who weren't permitted to participate in the regular sports program. At the end of the year the deputy warden gave Shorty George and me permission to have a banquet for them. We drew money from our own accounts and bought food and trophies. I stole the rest of what we needed from the kitchen, and we had a great banquet. As far as I know, we were the only inmates in the history of the institution who were given permission to go into that psychiatric ward (Top-6 they called it) whenever we wanted to. That's how much I had changed.

When I finished school I was reclassified to work in the gym instead of the kitchen, since I was spending all my free time there anyway. Because I was starring on all the varsity teams I didn't have to do much work. My main job was to pass out equipment each gym period and help sweep up after the period was over.

What I really wanted was the clerk's job in the gym. All he had to do was to set up the times for the various varsity sports and perform a few little administrative duties. The gym clerk at the time was doing life, so he wasn't going anywhere. Even though I liked the guy, I started thinking of ways to get him fired so I could take his job.

I misplaced some detail sheets in his office so that the officer on duty would think the clerk had messed up, and he was fired. I figured I was now the logical choice for the job, but I didn't know the clerk's job was set up on a black-white system. Whenever a black clerk left or was fired he was replaced with a white clerk, and vice versa. This clerk happened to be black, so they replaced him with a white guy. I still had to sweep up.

Even though I had decided to straighten myself out, I was doing a lot of crazy little things like drinking spud juice and "skating." Many of my friends didn't believe it when I said I was never coming back to prison. Another inmate and I stole thirteen pairs of new sneakers from the athletic director's office and sold them for ten bucks a pair. The athletic director, Dave Trippett, thought we were guilty and the officers questioned us but couldn't prove anything. Later word seeped out as the guys who were wearing the gym shoes told people where they had gotten them. By then it was too late; the shoes were worn out.

Eventually I got bored hanging around the gym and volunteered to work in the sanitation department. Sanitation workers were allowed to go out front to the main gate to pick up supplies, and sometimes they got to meet high administration officers, captains and inspectors who never came into the yard. I heard they even got to meet members of the parole board, so I decided to try to set myself up.

I did meet several members of the parole board while I was in the front hall waiting for supplies. Whenever I spotted one of them in the lobby, on a lunch break, I introduced myself. Unfortunately none of the people I talked to were on the board when I went for my hearing in March 1973.

I was living in the honor block at the time. (That was quite an accomplishment in itself, considering that I had spent five months in solitary confinement.) I knew that a lot of good reports had been written about me since I started playing sports, and I felt they should have been sufficient to overshadow the bad ones. I felt I had become a model prisoner and deserved a parole. Nevertheless I was scared to death when I went to my hearing.

They have so many rules in prison that it's awfully hard not to get into trouble. In fact you have to get into trouble in order to get out. If you don't get caught for anything, they accuse you of being con-wise. They'll say, "We have all these rules in here; do you mean to tell us you've been here for three years and you've never broken a single rule? You're too smart for us. You certainly are con-wise." So they flop you and make you wait another year before you can see the parole board again because they assume you must have been getting away with a lot.

Of course if you get into too much trouble, they'll flop you too. They get you either way. You have to break some of the rules in order to go home, but you can't break too many.

I knew the parole board had reports on everything I had done from the day I entered Jackson, but during my hearing they only read the bad parts aloud. I sat there like a dunce. I wanted to say, Why don't you read the good parts, too? But I knew they wouldn't like that, so I kept my mouth shut.

One member asked me, "Do you think you should be paroled?"

"Yes, I do," I said.

"Why do you think you should be paroled?" he asked. "What makes you think you're ready to be released, to go back to society and be a worthy citizen?"

I thought of all the good reports that various officers had assured me they had turned in and I replied, "When I came here, I did all those things you mentioned. I'm not going to lie and say I didn't. Everything everybody said about me was true at the time. When I came in here, I was going to be a rebellious person. I didn't know all that was going to come back to haunt me when I had to come before the parole board to ask for my release. I thought, when a guy's time was up, he was simply released and that was it. I didn't realize you could get out early by being good. When I learned you have to have respectable work reports and be involved in different activities around the institution, I began involving myself."

The guy just looked at me. He didn't smile or anything. He said, "Is that all you have to say?"

I nodded, and he handed me a slip of paper. It didn't say "paroled," it said "D–62," which meant "deferred for further discussion." I didn't know what to think. Later I was notified that I had been granted parole but wouldn't get out for at least ninety days. I guess they didn't want to parole me right away because of my bad early record. After more than three years in prison ninety days seemed like an awfully short time to wait.

Free at Last

As soon as I knew I was going home I became obsessed with the idea of playing baseball. Jimmy Karalla had a friend, Jimmy Butsicaris, who was supposedly a good friend of Billy Martin, then the manager of the Detroit Tigers. Karalla claimed that Butsicaris, who ran a bar in downtown Detroit, could help me if I wanted to play professional baseball. I kept after Karalla, hounding him to ask Butsicaris to get me a tryout with the Tigers.

In the middle of May I heard that the Tigers were planning to visit the prison. I told all my friends that Billy Martin was coming to Jackson just to see me. It wasn't that way at all, of course; the Tigers were coming to speak to all the inmates, and I didn't know whether Billy Martin would even be with them. But I kept thinking that this would be my chance.

I'll never forget that day, May 23, 1973. It was a dreary day, cold and rainy. It was one of the greatest days in my life.

Although Ron had no way of knowing it, the sequence of events that would eventually lead to his major league baseball career had actually begun a full year earlier, in May 1972, when Dave Trippett, the prison athletic director, invited Lew Matlin, the Detroit Tigers director of special events, to bring some ballplayers to the institution for a goodwill visit. Matlin was unable to make the necessary arrangements then, but he kept the invitation in mind, and in April 1973 he phoned Kermit Smith, who had succeeded Trippett, and scheduled a visit for May 23.

Meanwhile, unbeknownst to anyone in the Detroit Tigers organization, Jimmy Karalla had been bombarding Jimmy Butsicaris with telephone calls and letters extolling the athletic abilities of a young inmate named Ron LeFlore.

"I knew Ronnie was something special—I knew he was a helluva ballplayer," says Karalla, a forty-two-year-old who once worked as an assistant high school football coach and has now been paroled and lives in the Detroit area.

"I know my sports. I've played them all my life. If I hadn't gotten married so young, I probably would have tried to make the major leagues myself. I never could understand why the officials in the institution didn't notice Ronnie more than they did, why I, a convict, could spot something like that when all the other people up there couldn't.

"Once he signed everybody in there said, 'Oh yeah, we knew he was a heckuva ballplayer.' But nobody ever stuck their neck out for him. We *couldn't even get a stopwatch from the athletic department to time Ronnie. We had to borrow one from a teacher in the school, and he insisted on coming out on the field with us. He was afraid to let the stopwatch out of his sight."*

Karalla's perseverance paid off. Jimmy Butsicaris, co-owner of Detroit's popular Lindell Athletic Club, a bar frequented by sports celebrities and their followers, had been best man at Billy Martin's wedding and remained close to the Tiger manager. So, while Lew Matlin chauffeured Frank Howard and veteran Tiger radio announcer Ernie Harwell to Jackson Prison, Martin rode with Butsicaris. Along the way Butsicaris casually, cautiously, mentioned LeFlore.

"To be frank with you," Butsicaris admits, "in the twenty-seven years we've been associated with sports, my brother John and I have both been bugged by guys saying, I've got a cousin who's an outstanding ballplayer, or I know a guy who can really play ball.

"A couple of times I figured the guy knew what he was talking about, so I tried to do him a favor. When Mayo Smith was managing the Tigers, an entertainer friend of mine saw a guy pitch in the Ozarks and said he was tremendous, so I brought the kid to Detroit and got him a tryout with the Tigers. I made a complete ass of myself. The kid didn't know how to stand on the rubber or how to deliver the ball. It was embarrassing for everybody, especially for me. After that I kind of shied away from that stuff.

*"Guys would tell me about ballplayers they had
discovered, and I'd say, Yeah, fine, I'll see what I can
do for you. Then I'd forget about it. Normally, in
America, if a kid is any kind of ballplayer at all,
somebody is going to find him before he gets very
old.*

*"So I didn't pay too much attention when
Karalla first started calling me about this kid,
LeFlore. I told them to send a letter to the Tigers, to
the scouting department or to Jim Campbell. I told
them to go ahead and use my name. Karalla said
they had already tried that and nothing had
happened. Karalla kept calling me. They have a rule
in Jackson that the inmates have to call collect, and
you wouldn't believe what my phone bill was that
one month. I figured I had better get off my ass and
go up there to see them, just to get them off my back.*

*"On the way to the penitentiary I hesitated to
tell Billy about this kid. I knew what he would say. I
had already mentioned a couple of guys to him, and
he'd said, 'Yeah, Jimmy, I know, I hear the same
thing all the time.'*

*"Finally I said, 'There's a guy up here in Jackson
I'd like you to take a look at if you get a chance.'
Billy kind of laughed, and I didn't say anything
more about it."*

Lew Matlin and his contingent arrived at the
prison first. While Frank Howard and Ernie Harwell
went inside to mingle with the inmates, Matlin and
assistant athletic director Bob Sudberry waited at the
main gate for Butsicaris and Martin. As they waited
Sudberry told Matlin about a great young athlete in

the institution, a fellow Sudberry thought might be good enough to play professional football or basketball—or baseball. His name was Ron LeFlore.

"I happened to be looking at a copy of the prison newspaper at the time," Matlin recalls, "and I noticed that LeFlore's name wasn't mentioned in any of the articles or in the box scores on the sports page. 'If this guy LeFlore is so good,' I said, 'how come he isn't playing on your baseball team?'

"Sudberry explained that LeFlore was going to be released on parole in August and was living in a facility removed from the general population of the prison, getting himself prepared to go home. Then Sudberry went to make a telephone call. A few minutes later a prison vehicle pulled up and a muscular, good-looking young black man got out. It was LeFlore.

"Martin arrived at about the same time, and Sudberry introduced Ron to Billy. Later we were standing in the yard talking when all of a sudden it seemed as if a circle of inmates had formed around LeFlore and Martin. One fellow, a big white dude, yelled, 'Hey, Martin, give the boy a chance!' I later found out it was Jimmy Karalla, a friend of Jimmy Butsicaris. Anyway, Martin looked around at all those guys, saw he was outmatched, and said to Ron, 'Son, whenever you're in Tiger Stadium, come out and I'll give you a workout.'

"A few weeks later, on June 15, I happened to be in Billy Martin's office in the clubhouse a few hours before the game, checking with him on some speaking engagements I had lined up, when the phone rang.

"Billy answered it, then put his hand over the receiver. 'Who's Ron LeFlore?' he asked.

"I said, 'He's that young man you met at Jackson Prison and invited to work out.'

" 'Oh, yeah, by God that's right,' Billy said.

"He uncovered the phone and said, 'When you coming down, Ronnie?'

"The voice on the phone said, 'Tomorrow.' "

I got my furlough the weekend of June 15–17. For the first time since I had been arrested and locked up in the Wayne County Jail three and a half years before, I was going to be free—for forty-eight hours.

My father had bought a car by then, and he picked me up late Friday afternoon. Saturday morning we went to the Lindell AC to wait for Jimmy Butsicaris. I was really excited. It was my twenty-third birthday, and I couldn't imagine a better present. Even though it was only 9:30 in the morning, I ordered a beer. It was the first real alcohol I had tasted since I went to prison.

When we got to Tiger Stadium, Butsicaris took us right into the clubhouse and into Billy Martin's office. The Tigers were playing the Minnesota Twins that day in the national TV Game of the Week. Billy told the clubhouse man, John Hand, to get me a uniform and then introduced me to some of the players. Right away everybody began giving me things.

The first guy Billy introduced me to, Art Fowler, the pitching coach, gave me an extra baseball glove he had in his locker. I met Frank Howard again, and he gave me a couple of bats. Willie Horton gave me a couple of bats, too, and I got a couple from Al Kaline.

After I had dressed, Billy took me onto the field where

the extra men, the guys who weren't going to be playing that day, like Frank Howard and Ike Brown and Tony Taylor, were taking batting practice. Art Fowler was pitching and Billy told me to go right into the batting cage and start hitting.

I stepped up to the plate, swung as hard as I could at the first pitch, and missed the ball completely. However, I don't think I missed another ball the rest of the day.

I was gripping the bat real tight, and after the first round of batting practice I noticed that my hands were starting to blister. I didn't know anything about batting gloves. I had never heard of putting pine tar on a bat. Someone once told me you were supposed to grip the bat so tight that you could hear a squeaking sound when you turned your hands, so that was what I did. I didn't realize I was rubbing my hands raw; I really tore them up.

Al Kaline was pitching batting practice when I got up for the second time, and again they told me to take fifteen or twenty swings even though the other guys were taking only six. I hit a few balls into the upper deck, and I heard Frank Howard say, "He's hitting 'em up into the upper deck the way Willie hits 'em." Being compared to Willie Horton made me feel good.

I was trying so hard to impress the organization with the fact that I was capable of playing professional baseball that I was pulling everything to left field. But I was hitting the ball solidly even if they were all going to left field. Most of the balls I hit would have been base hits in a game.

I later learned that Billy had called Mr. Campbell, the general manager, and that he watched me for a while from his private box down the rightfield line. A few of the reporters on the field, waiting for the game to start, tried to talk to me, but Billy told them they couldn't because I wasn't part of the organization. However, I heard several people say, "Hey, he can really hit that ball."

After batting practice Art Fowler told me to shag a few fly balls in center field. I guess they wanted to see if I could throw. When I got to center field Mickey Stanley was already there. I didn't know exactly what to do or where to throw the ball, but Mickey said, "Just watch me and throw the ball where I do."

Stanley caught the first fly ball and threw it to third base, so I caught the next one and threw to third, too. I threw it hard. "God, you've got a strong arm," Stanley said. "You throw the ball better than I do." We took turns shagging fly balls, and I kept making perfect throws, one-hoppers, to third base. I was playing a little deeper than Mickey and I was taking my time. I didn't know how to throw properly, how to take a step and get something on the ball when I released it. I would stop still, put my foot down, and then throw the ball. Stanley told me to field the ball on the move so I could get more velocity on my throws. I tried it, but it felt awkward because I had never thrown like that before, and I went back to throwing from a standstill.

After practice I took a shower while the Tigers got ready to play the Minnesota Twins. But they seemed more interested in me than in the Twins. They seemed genuinely thrilled at what they had seen. Duke Sims said I looked like a real good ballplayer. Jimmy Butsicaris told me later that a lot of players approached him or Billy Martin while I was in the shower and said they were very impressed with me. Al Kaline told Butsicaris that from what he had seen, I was better than anybody the Tigers had at Toledo, their top farm club at the time. He said if it was up to him, he'd sign me right away. Billy Martin had talked to Jim Campbell by then and said the club wanted me to work out again, at Butzel Field in northwest Detroit, in front of their scouts, as soon as possible.

When I returned to prison I contacted Bill Lajoie, the man in charge of the Tigers' scouting department, and told him the procedure for getting me another furlough. The following weekend I was granted a furlough, a one-day, eight-hour pass, and on Saturday morning my father picked me up again.

By now I was beginning to believe I was going to get to play professional baseball. Riding to Detroit I thought how I would show them what I could do at the workout. Then, as we reached the outskirts of Detroit on Interstate 94, my father's car threw a rod.

I was sick. I figured I was going to miss the workout and the whole thing was going to fall through. My career would be over before it got started. Standing on the highway alongside the car, I kept yelling at my father to do something—anything—to get the car started. Of course, there was nothing he could do. It was about a quarter after nine, and I was supposed to be at Butzel Field at ten o'clock. We couldn't see a gas station or a telephone, so I started to hitchhike. A factory worker who had just gotten off the midnight shift picked us up and drove us all the way to Butzel Field. I never knew his name, but I certainly was grateful.

The workout had already begun when we arrived. But Bill Lajoie and Ed Katalinas, who are responsible for signing all the Tigers' new young players, stopped everything and held a special workout for me. My hands were still sore from the week before, and I didn't have a uniform. I wore prison dungarees and a short-sleeve shirt. But that didn't hinder me.

Lajoie teamed me with a guy who was supposed to be the fastest player there, and I beat him by ten yards in the sixty-yard dash. They clocked me in 6.2 seconds. They put me up against the best pitcher there when I took batting practice. I hit the ball well again, this time both to left field and to right field. Katalinas and Lajoie said they liked my inside-out swing. They sent me to the outfield and told me to throw a few balls. They seemed very pleased.

They took down my parents' address and telephone number and asked if I wanted to sign a professional baseball contract when I got out of prison. Just like that! I couldn't believe it. I never expected it. I figured that even if I did well in the workout I would have to go back to Butzel every week for a while after I got out of prison, until they could see I was progressing. But they asked me if I wanted to sign a professional baseball contract—right there on the spot. I was stunned. My father was stunned. I was so excited I could hardly say yes.

"Ron was a lightning bolt," declares Ed Katalinas, who signed Al Kaline and a number of other Tiger stars. "I'm not normally a one-looker, but as far as I was concerned he was the biggest chunk of raw talent I had ever seen. He was the kind of boy you build a championship team around.

"You look and look for ballplayers like that, and you wonder, Where are they? To find one, like Ron, right in front of your nose—it was really something.

"The first thing we look for in a boy is the body. Ron definitely had the ideal physical build. His speed was another plus factor. He had two plus factors going for him right away.

"We had batting practice, and he hit some balls

out of the ball park; we checked his arm and found it was more than satisfactory. Arm, body, speed, power—what else is there to look for?"

The Tigers have been holding informal tryouts camps at Butzel Field every Saturday morning since 1971. Over the years the sessions have produced very little talent. In fact, of all the kids who have shown up uninvited with dreams of becoming big league ballplayers, only five have ever signed professional contracts. Only one of those ever made it as far as spring training camp with the Tigers. Ron, of course, was invited—but Ed Katalinas and Bill Lajoie weren't expecting much from him either.

"When I heard what had happened at Tiger Stadium I was skeptical because it sounded too good to be true," Lajoie admits. "So I had Ron run against a player whom I knew to be the fastest there. When Ron got about twenty-five yards from the starting point, it was obvious he was going to accelerate past the other young man. I couldn't believe the fluidness of his running and the power of his stride. I could recall seeing only two other ballplayers with Ron's size and build who could run like that. One, Carroll Hardy, became a big leaguer in the 1960s and also played in the National Football League; the other was a fullback at Miami of Ohio University named Boxcar Beatty."

Katalinas and Lajoie weren't the only ones who were impressed with Ron LeFlore that morning. Another scout, Mark Esper, employed by the Oakland A's, happened to be in the stands, and he asked LeFlore to write his name and address on a card and pass it back to him. Bill Lajoie still doesn't speak to Mark Esper because of that incident.

However, according to Billy Martin, the Tiger front office was not all that eager to take a chance on Ron at first.

"They weren't too excited about signing him," maintains Martin, who was fired by Detroit later that summer and now manages the New York Yankees. "I brought him to the park to work out and I was crazy about him. Mickey Stanley, Norm Cash, Al Kaline—all the other guys liked him, too. They said, Billy, he's sensational!

"I told Jim Campbell that if he saw the same player walking down the street and didn't know where he'd come from or what he had done, he'd sign him for $100,000 in a second. Ronnie showed that much raw ability.

"But they were a little hesitant. One guy in the organization, and I don't want to name him, said, 'But Billy, he's in jail.' And I asked that guy, 'Where do you think you got Gates Brown from— kindergarten?'"

Tiger General Manager Jim Campbell, who as farm director was involved in signing Gates Brown out of the Ohio State Reformatory in 1960, denies any such reluctance regarding LeFlore.

"That's absolutely not the way it was!" Campbell insists. "We were never at any point reluctant to sign Ron because of his background. We demonstrated our confidence in a fellow who has served his time when we signed Gates Brown—long before anybody heard of Ron LeFlore. And Gates Brown conducted

in every way like a professional athlete
It was because of the fine example Gates had
we were willing to give Ron LeFlore a

*...on had served his time, and he had a good
record in prison. He was highly recommended by the
people in the prison system. He paid his penalty. I
don't know how many other organizations have
signed players who have been in trouble or in jail,
but we have, and we've had good results. I'm proud
of that record.*

*"Billy Martin did say this kid had talent. He
said he was strong and could really run. And the
other players who saw him were impressed. Bill
Lajoie made arrangements for him to work out, and
from then on the matter was in the hands of our
scouting department. The final decision to sign Ron
LeFlore was made by Bill Lajoie after he had worked
him out at Butzel Field."*

*Another thing that impressed the Tigers was the
fact that Ron had taken two IQ tests when he first
entered prison. One placed his IQ at 128, the other
at 130.*

When I returned to prison I called my mother as often
as I could, telling her to call the Tigers—Bill Lajoie, Ed
Katalinas, and Jim Campbell—to make sure they didn't forget their promise to sign me as soon as I got out. I told her
to call the State Department of Corrections in Lansing to try
to find out exactly when I would be released. My parole date
was August 2, but I heard that if the parole board knew I had
a job waiting, there was a chance I might be released before
then.

The Oakland A's were interested in me, and Frank Quillici, the manager of the Minnesota Twins, had told Jimmy Butsicaris that the Twins would probably sign me if Detroit didn't. I thought I could get them all bidding for me —I figured if I started a bidding war, I'd get a big bonus. I told my mother to tell Jim Campbell that Minnesota and Oakland and a lot of other clubs were interested in me.

I was living in a parole camp outside the walls of the prison, and I asked Kermit Smith, the athletic director, to send me balls and bats so I could continue to work out.

There was an old baseball field at the parole camp that hadn't been used for years. I got a lawn mower and cut the grass and dug up all the weeds, and I hoed up the baseline so I could practice running from home plate to first base. I was working then in the parole camp kitchen; after I had cooked breakfast for the other guys I'd work on my baseball field the rest of the day. I leveled the field as best I could and persuaded some other inmates to hit fly balls to me in the afternoon once they got off work. I had guys hitting balls to me all over the outfield. I took a little batting practice, too —when I could find somebody who would pitch to me. But the other inmates weren't that interested, so most of what I did, I did by myself.

I could have run away from the prison camp if I had wanted to. Many times on the baseball field, with nobody around, I thought how easy it would be to walk off. But where would I be if I had gotten five more years after serving three and a half?

Other inmates in the camp knew I had a chance to play pro ball. One Saturday, while we were watching a baseball game on TV, I said, "See those players? Next year you guys are going to be watching a baseball game on TV and you're going to see me because I'm going to be in the big leagues in one year's time." They didn't believe me, and I really didn't believe it myself. But the more they insisted I would never make it, the more I insisted I would.

I had everything ready to go. My parents had brought me clothes to wear home, and I didn't have much to pack. After dinner on the first of July the parole clerk informed me I was going home in the morning. I thought he was kidding —I didn't believe him until I saw my name on the detail sheet, with instructions for the guard on the night shift to wake me up early the next morning so I could be processed to leave.

When I stepped outside those walls on July 2, 1973, I still couldn't believe it. I stood on the sidewalk before the institution for fifteen minutes, just breathing fresh air. I was twenty-three years old and I was starting life all over again. "I'm free," I kept sighing, "I'm free at last."

Hit the Ball and Run

11

I didn't give the Tigers a chance to change their mind. My father and I drove straight from the prison to the ball park, where my parole officer and his supervisor were waiting in Jim Campbell's office to explain the procedures the ball club and I would have to go through. I had been released a month early because the Tigers assured the parole board they had a job waiting, and I was placed in the custody of the ball club. After all the rules had been explained I signed my first professional baseball contract: $5,-000 in bonus money and $500 a month for what remained of the 1973 season. Finally I was going to be making money legally.

Instead of sending me to a rookie league, as they usually do with a kid with no experience, the Tigers started me out on their farm team in Clinton, Iowa, in the Class A Midwest League. Bill Lajoie, who was to drive me to my first assignment, asked when I wanted to leave. The Fourth of July was a couple of days away, and since I hadn't been home in three and a half years I told him I'd like to wait until after the holiday.

I had approximately $3,600 in my prison account when I was paroled—money I made working in the kitchen, money my parents had given me, and—mostly—money I accumulated by wheeling and dealing, which I'd slip to my mother or brother whenever they came to visit. (They'd deposit it in my account as if it was coming from them.) But the prison officials gave me only $100 when I was released. It's against the rules to leave prison with more than $100 in your pocket; they figure that if you have more money than that, you'll go on a binge to celebrate your release and maybe end up back inside. So they give you only $100, and your parole officer gets the rest to dole out as he sees fit.

The Tigers didn't give me all my bonus money, either, because my contract still had to be approved by the national association that oversees the minor leagues. They gave me $2,500, and I gave most of that to my mother to hold. Then I went downtown and bought myself some clothes.

I had grown in prison, and I had to buy a whole new wardrobe. I took $800 downtown and spent it all in two hours. I really splurged. I didn't know enough to go to the cheaper stores, and $800 is nothing when you have nothing to start with and you're buying only high-priced clothes.

I was so excited at finally being free that I wanted to see all my old friends right away. That night I went to a bar where several of them hung out, but after a couple of drinks I was dead tired. The guy with me was just starting to party when I said, "Hey, man, take me home. I'm falling asleep." I was accustomed to being locked up every night at 9:30— and the lights would go out at ten, so there wasn't much sense in staying awake after that. It took me a couple of months to get used to staying up late and being able to do whatever I wanted to do.

On the morning of July 5 Bill Lajoie and I left for Decatur, Illinois, where the Clinton team was playing. There were so many things I had wanted to do when I got home, so many things I had thought about doing while I was in prison—and I hardly had time to do any of them. That was the best thing that could have happened to me! There's no telling what might have happened if I'd had time to hang around the old neighborhood and my old friends. I was afraid I might have been picked up by the police again, or I might have been with friends who got picked up for something. Either way, I would have been right back in prison. But I wasn't home long enough to get involved, and by the time I came home from Clinton at the end of the season, I had made new friends and begun a whole new life.

When we reached Decatur, Bill took me to the motel where the team was staying and introduced me to the manager, Jim Leyland. He explained the different rules he had —curfew and what time to be at the ball park—and told me to shave my mustache. Then he took me around the motel and introduced me to some of the other players.

When we got to the ball park none of the players talked to me. When I walked by they'd say, "Hi, how ya doing?" but that was all. Everybody seemed skeptical of me, like they didn't know quite how to take me. (I later learned that Jim Leyland had told them about my background and said he thought it would be best if they left me alone at first and let me feel my way.) I was sitting alone in the clubhouse when Eddie Glynn, a lefthanded pitcher, came over and asked, "You from prison?" Just like that.

"Yeah," I said, "I've been in prison."

"What did you do?"

He sat down, and I began telling him all about it. The other guys saw that, and from then on everything was fine. In fact a bunch of us went out that night after the game, shot a little pool, and got drunk. At least I did; I wasn't used to drinking anything but spud juice, and after a couple of beers and a couple of shots, I was in bad shape.

On our way back to the motel—it must have been about one o'clock in the morning—we walked by a clothing store that had several fur and leather coats in the window. We stopped to look, and I said, "If we were in Detroit, and I wasn't playing baseball, I would throw a brick through this window and grab a couple of these coats."

I looked up and down the street, checking for police cars, and said, "I should do it anyway. What do you guys think? Let's knock this window out and get these clothes."

They were all looking at me, and someone said, "Oh, no, I don't think so." They were all probably scared of me for being just out of prison.

"Hey, I'm only joking," I said. "I just got out of prison and I don't want to go back. I can't afford to do anything like that. I'm trying to better myself, not downgrade myself." They laughed and we went on down the street.

We got a couple of six packs of beer and sat up until four o'clock in the morning, smoking cigarettes, drinking beer, and talking about the things we had done. I told them a little about my background—and I guess I shocked the shit out of them. They didn't think anyone did things like that. I told them about dope addicts and being shot at, but they had a hard time believing it because they hadn't been brought up in an environment like that. Their lives were totally different from mine. They lived the kinds of lives I would have to live if I was going to stay out of prison. I decided to try to learn what I could from them, and eventually I got very close to a lot of my teammates at Clinton.

> *Clinton Manager Jim Leyland admits that he was a little leery of Ron at first.*
>
> *"When I was told I was going to get him, frankly, I didn't know what to expect," Leyland recalls. "I presumed you could have all sorts of special problems with a kid on parole. Could he cross state lines with the ball club? Did I have to keep him out of bars and pool halls? What happened if a brawl broke out on the field and he piled on?*
>
> *"As it turned out, I didn't have any problems with Ron at all. I guess the prison experience must have helped him rather than hurt."*

Because of my background the press began paying attention to me right away. I was on TV, people from NBC in New York did a little skit with me, I was interviewed by *Time* magazine. I received a lot of local publicity too, not only in Clinton but everywhere we played. I had never been questioned like that before, I had never been on TV, and I was uptight—I didn't know what to say. Reporters would ask me about my past or my lack of playing experience, and I'd say yes, or no, or yeah. I wanted to explain myself better, but I didn't know how.

Shortly after I started getting the publicity I received a vicious hate letter. The writer called me "boy" and "nigger" and said, "You should never have been given a chance to play baseball or do anything else because you're nothing but an ex-con." After I had read the letter I passed it around the clubhouse and let everyone else read it. I think that made them feel I was a part of them, part of the team.

Another incident helped too. The first time we played Cedar Rapids a fight broke out on the field and both benches emptied. Cedar Rapids had a player, Freddie Nims, who was supposed to be the toughest guy in the league; he had challenged everybody, and everybody was afraid of him. When the fight started I was the first one out of our dugout. I ran straight to home plate, where Nims was standing, and looked him right in the face. I guess he had heard about my being in prison and was afraid to mess with me because he turned and walked away. And when he walked away the entire Cedar Rapids team walked away. I think that drew the guys on my team closer to me; they knew I would stand up and fight for them, and they knew I was the toughest guy on the team.

But none of this helped me play better baseball. There were times during that summer at Clinton when I wished I hadn't been released from prison a month early, times I wished the Tigers had waited until 1974 to send me to the minor leagues. Minor league baseball was totally different from the baseball I was accustomed to playing. In prison I was so much better than the guys I played with and against that I thought the game was easy. I thought all you had to do was play. When I got to professional ball, even Class A baseball, I realized how wrong I had been.

Clinton was in first place when I joined them. It was an excellent team. I was a new outfielder on a team where all the other outfielders were hitting over .300. I was with the club seven or eight days before I even got into a game.

The first time I went to bat I got an infield hit. I was jammed on the pitch, hit the ball a couple of hops to the third baseman, and beat it out. The next day the headline in the local paper said, "LeFlore Batting 1.000." I went 0 for 17 after that.

I was scared at the plate, I'll admit it. And I looked ridiculous at times. In prison I saw curve balls only once in a great while, but in the minor leagues I saw hundreds of them. Most of them weren't even good curve balls, but they sure fooled me. I'd be standing at the plate, the pitcher would throw the ball hard and inside, and I'd jump out of the way, thinking it was a fastball. And the umpire would call a strike.

We played mostly night games at Clinton and I had never played under the lights. They had other uses for the floodlights in Jackson.

Clinton was altogether different from the area in which I grew up. There weren't the factories or the smoke and pollution of Detroit; just clean country air. There were no drug addicts, either—I didn't see one the whole time. The people were different; they were clean. I really enjoyed Clinton, the people, and the country air.

I was invited to a lot of parties, and many times I was the only black player on the team who was invited. Of course many people wanted to pick my brain to find out what caused me to go to jail. I didn't mind; I was willing to tell anyone what had happened to me. I wasn't embarrassed or ashamed.

I moved into an apartment with two white teammates, Jim Harris and David Kuhn. I think Billy Baldwin and Art James assumed that because they were black I'd live with them. But Jim and Dave invited me to move in, and since they had a big apartment on the main street, near the ball park, I accepted.

We got along fine. There were two bedrooms in the

apartment, one with a big bed, the other with twin beds. We flipped coins to see who was going to sleep where. I won; I got the bedroom with the big bed and the shower.

By this time I had been on TV in Clinton and been written up in the local paper several times. A number of the girls around town who heard about me began coming to the apartment, and we had little parties going all the time. There weren't many black families in Clinton, so most of the girls were white—which was a new experience for me. Aside from the short time I went to Catholic school, I had never met many white girls; there hadn't been any around my old neighborhood. But the color of the girls in Clinton made no difference to me. If a girl was willing to be with me, or have sex with me, that was all that mattered. And a lot of them were willing.

When articles about me began appearing in the Detroit papers, my old girl friend, Deborah Hutchins (whom I now live with), found out I hadn't been in the army and got in touch with me. She flew to Clinton for a few days, and we got together again. But that didn't stop me from messing with the girls in Clinton.

In Detroit the Tiger front office was paying more than casual attention to Ron's budding career.

"I felt we had a moral responsibility to help him get off on the right foot," General Manager Jim Campbell explains. "We realized that coming out of prison would be especially difficult in Ron's case because he wasn't going to be just another guy going to work in a factory. He was going to work on a stage, where the fans, the newspapers, and national TV would all be watching him. It certainly was a

different atmosphere from that most fellows encounter when they're released from prison. We felt a responsibility to him, to the state of Michigan, and to baseball."

Meanwhile, as word of Ron's signing spread, the Tigers began receiving queries from convicts and friends of convicts around the country asking if they could try out, too. The Tigers invited them all to Butzel Field when they were released from prison— but they haven't yet found another Ron LeFlore.

I was out of jail and I had a job, but I wasn't rich. I was making $500 a month, but after deductions and after I had paid my share of the rent ($80 a month), I didn't have a lot of money left. I hadn't received the rest of my bonus; the national association was taking time to investigate me because of my prison record. And my parole officer wouldn't give me the rest of the money from my prison account because he didn't think I needed it.

Instead of riding back to the apartment after a game, I would sometimes walk home, looking at the stores and thinking how easy it would be to break in. Most of the stores didn't have burglar alarms as far as I could see, and I figured it would be simple.

I pushed the idea out of my mind. Then, when the rest of my bonus money arrived, I had no reason to think about stealing anymore.

We won the Midwest League championship that year. There was champagne for us in the clubhouse, and I doused the general manager, Fritz Colschen. He was a stern guy— the other players acted as if they were afraid of him—but I poured champagne over his head. Later we had a team party and everybody was dumping pitchers of beer on one another. I was on the telephone long distance to my mother, telling her I would be a few days late getting to Detroit, when two teammates snuck up behind me and poured two pitchers over my head. I think the other guys were afraid I would get mad. There was no chance of that; it was too much fun being a winner. I had never experienced anything like it in my life.

In Detroit the Tigers had fired Billy Martin a few weeks earlier, and I didn't know what to expect. Since Martin was the one who gave me permission to work out and got me signed, I was afraid I'd be forgotten with him gone. After all I hit only .277 in thirty-two games at Clinton and stole only two bases. However, at the end of the season the Tigers sent me to their Dunedin team in the Florida Instructional League, where they send all the top prospects in their farm system every fall for intensified training. Immediately I began to feel better. If they thought enough of me to send me to Dunedin, they weren't likely to forget me.

That fall a writer and photographer from *Sports Illustrated* came to Dunedin to see Danny Meyer and me. Danny had hit .396 at Bristol in 1972, the highest batting average anywhere in professional baseball, and the Tigers were high on him. The photographer took pictures of both of us, and the writer said the article would be about both Danny Meyer and me. I told my friends I was going to be in *Sports Illustrated*; I called my mother, and she alerted a lot of people in Detroit. Then the article appeared and it was all Danny Meyer—my name wasn't mentioned. I made up my mind I was going to have to do something to let people know I could play, too.

That fall I met Laura, who was living in Florida. We

became friends, and the following spring, while I was at minor league training camp, she drove to Lakeland regularly. When the Tigers assigned me to play at Lakeland that summer, in the Class A Florida State League, she moved there and got a job so she could be with me all the time.

I sent her to a new apartment complex near the ball park to rent me a place to live. At first she told the apartment manager that she was Mrs. Ron LeFlore. Laura's white and the manager didn't know I was black, and he said fine. The next day, when I showed up with her, he claimed he had no vacancies. Some southerners don't like the idea of a black guy going with a white girl. But he relented and agreed to rent me a two-bedroom apartment.

Hoot Evers, who runs the Tiger farm system, used to say, "You're gonna be cold stone turkey in the market," meaning I was going to get lynched or something. They did have a Ku Klux Klan rally in Lakeland one night, a few blocks from where we lived, and let me tell you—I was scared.

From the start of spring training I was hitting the ball better than I had the year before. I wasn't bailing out so much on breaking balls—instead of stepping way out of the batter's box and swinging and missing by five or six feet, I was hanging in there most of the time. And I was beginning to steal bases even though I still didn't know how to slide. I'd jump in the air, put both feet out, and barrel into the base as hard as I could. I was getting the knack of playing the outfield, too.

The Tigers' minor league training complex is right next to the major league training camp, on an abandoned air base where pilots were trained during World War II. Whenever I wasn't practicing or playing an exhibition game I'd watch the Class AA or the Class AAA players. If there was an exhibition game in Marchant Stadium, I'd watch the major leaguers play. I watched everything, trying to learn as much as I could. Compared to most guys in the minor leagues, I still didn't know a thing about playing baseball.

Before the 1974 season began I told Hoot Evers, "I'm going to lead this Florida State League in every category there is." I almost did, too; I had a fantastic year at Lakeland. I led the league with a .339 batting average and was first in runs scored and stolen bases (forty-two). I led the league in hitting every week but one, when my roomie, Billy Baldwin, snuck ahead of me. My batting average never dropped below .330 the entire season. There were only five or six games—out of ninety-two—in which I didn't get at least one hit. I was running all the time, stealing so many bases that I was actually learning how to slide. I was still making errors in the outfield, but they were aggressive errors that came from my lack of experience.

In June Hoot Evers visited Lakeland, and I asked for a raise. He gave me one, too—to $750 a month—and he made a deal: Every time Billy Baldwin and I got five hits between us in a game, he would buy us both a steak dinner. I told Baldwin, "All you gotta do is get one hit a game, and I'll take care of the rest."

Hoot was there for a week, and we got five hits every game for six straight days. That was six straight steak dinners. Then he called the deal off—he said he couldn't afford to continue.

The Lakeland ball club had an arrangement whereby a player would get a certificate for a free steak dinner at Bonanza every time he hit a home run. I wasn't hitting many home runs, but I was doing so many other things to help the club that Frank Decker, the general manager, gave me a lot of those certificates anyway. I hardly ever spent my own money on food.

All those hits and stolen bases really helped my confidence. In July I thought it was time I was promoted to Montgomery in the Class AA Southern League, the next step up the ladder in the Tiger farm system. I told a reporter from the Lakeland paper that the pitching in the Florida State League wasn't helping me any more. I thought I was more advanced than the guys I was playing with and against, that I ought to be promoted so I could see better pitching and improve as a ballplayer. Hoot Evers was pissed at me for saying it, but that was the way I felt.

Whenever I made a mistake my manager, Stubby Overmire, would call me aside and say, "Look, Ron, you've always got to think ahead, to anticipate the situation before it happens." Stubby told me to study everything about the game: opposing pitchers and opposing hitters, how different fielders played me when I was at bat, whose arm was strong and whose wasn't. I had never paid attention to those things before; I didn't know it was necessary. I thought all you had to do was hit the ball and run.

I still had to report to my parole officer every month. The parole board had transferred my papers to Florida and appointed a parole officer for me in Lakeland. It was a pain in the ass to have to go to his office every month. Since I was playing so well and causing no problems, I felt my parole should be dropped. Instead I almost got into trouble again.

A retiree had lived formerly in the apartment I rented, and his pension check was sent to our address by mistake. One of my teammates stole the check from the mailbox. He was caught trying to cash it, and he told the police I had given it to him.

An investigator came to the apartment. I told him I

never went near the mailbox, that I had all my mail sent to the ball park. (The only letters I received were from my mother, anyway.) "If that guy stole the check," I said, "he stole it on his own.

"I'm on parole," I explained. "Why would I get involved in something like that when I know that if I have to go to court for *anything*, it's an automatic violation and I go right back to prison?" I said I was willing to take a polygraph test or whatever was necessary to prove my innocence.

My parole officer called me in. "Look," I told him, "I'm making good money; I don't have to steal somebody's check. I'm able to take care of my bills, I'm able to save a little money, I'm not having any problems. Why would I risk blowing everything over a little pension check?" I never heard any more about the matter.

On July 22, I got my wish. Stubby Overmire called me into his office and told me I was being promoted—not to Montgomery, but all the way to Evansville, Indiana, the top Tiger farm club, in the Class AAA American Association. Now I was really going to get an opportunity to show the Detroit organization what I could do! I got Laura to pack my stuff and I caught the first plane to Evansville.

When I had been there about a week, another outfielder, Smokey Robinson, was sent to Montgomery, and I made arrangements to move out of the motel and into his apartment. I bought about $80 worth of groceries that afternoon. My brother Gerald and his girl friend had come to Evansville to visit, and I told them they could stay in the apartment, too. After the game that night we all moved in.

The next morning the general manager of the Evansville team, Tom Coyne, got me out of bed at a quarter to ten.

"You're going to Detroit," he said.

"Going to Detroit?" I mumbled, still half asleep. "What for?"

"To play center field."

Tony Kubek and Me, on National TV

Things were happening so fast I hardly had time to think. I flew to Detroit to sign a major league contract for the minimum $15,000 salary, then I flew to Milwaukee on August 1 to join the Tigers. I checked into the Pfister Hotel, threw my suitcase on the bed, and called manager Ralph Houk. I had heard about Ralph from players in the minor leagues who had been with the Tigers in spring training, but I had never met him. I didn't know what to expect when I went to his room. Hell, I didn't even know why I was in Milwaukee.

The regular Tiger centerfielder, Mickey Stanley, had broken his hand, but I couldn't picture myself as his replacement—not yet. I assumed I would sit on the bench for the rest of the season and pinch-hit or pinch-run once in a while. I was stunned when Ralph shook my hand and said, "You're starting tonight. You're going to be my centerfielder and you're going to lead off.

"I've never seen you play, but I've heard a lot about you and I like what I've heard," Houk went on. "I know you don't have a lot of baseball experience, but regardless what happens remember you're going to be playing. If you make mistakes, you're going to get a chance to redeem yourself. Don't worry about that. Don't get down on yourself if you don't do everything right away. I'm going to give you a chance."

The Tigers had assigned me a roommate, Marvin Lane, another young outfielder from Detroit. He was waiting when I got to our room, and I asked him to fill me in. I was going to be leadoff batter and I didn't know who was pitching for Milwaukee that night. Shit, I didn't even know who was on their team! I knew the names of major league superstars like Johnny Bench and Cesar Cedeno, but I had never learned who was on what team. I had only worried about my own career.

Marvin told me that Jim Slaton was pitching for Milwaukee and warned me, "He's got a helluva curve ball. You're gonna see it about seventy-five percent of the time, too."

I was in a daze when I got to Milwaukee's County Stadium. It seemed as if there were a heavy fog all around me and I was the only guy on the field. I knelt in the on-deck circle, waiting my first turn at bat, and barely heard the people in the stands behind the dugout yelling, "Go back to jail, Jailbird!"

My first time up, Slaton threw me his goddamn curve and I jumped out of the batter's box. I thought for sure the ball was going to hit me; I had never seen a curve ball break the way his did. Slaton struck me out three times that night —my first three times at bat in the big leagues. In the eighth inning I grounded out to the third baseman. I could feel my knees shaking; I was scared to death. Three balls were hit to me in the outfield and I caught all three, though I went through such a routine getting to the ball that I made them all look like circus catches.

Even though we won, 2–0 (Woodie Fryman pitched a one-hitter), I felt that I had made a fool of myself. When the team got back to the hotel I went into the bar off the lobby, determined to get good and drunk. As I looked for an empty stool I heard someone call my name. It was Al Kaline.

"Ronnie, come on, sit down, I've been waiting for you," he said. He ordered me a drink and we sat there until the bar closed, just Al Kaline and me, talking baseball. He told me about some of the pitchers around the league and pointed out a few things I had done wrong in that night's game. He told me all sorts of things about baseball that nobody had ever mentioned to me before.

It was a thrill to talk with him. Al Kaline was only a name when I was growing up—a name in a different world. Who would have thought our paths would ever cross? Now I found myself listening to every word he said, trying to absorb some of the knowledge he had accumulated over the years.

The decision to bring Ron to the big leagues had been reached only after an expensive long-distance debate in which the Tiger hierarchy—Jim Campbell, Ralph Houk, Hoot Evers, Stubby Overmire, and Ron's manager at Evansville, Fred Hatfield— carefully weighed the pros and cons.

It was not a unanimous verdict. Hatfield, who had seen Ron play only a few games, favored Leon

Roberts, a more experienced outfielder who was enjoying an excellent year at AAA level. Evers, who as Tiger farm director had followed LeFlore's career closely from the beginning, admits, "I thought we were insane bringing him up to the big leagues so quickly."

But Overmire convinced the others that Ron was talented and intelligent enough to overcome his glaring lack of experience, and Ralph Houk agreed to give the twenty-four-year-old ex-convict a chance.

After my dismal debut I was afraid the Tigers would send me back to the minor leagues in spite of what Ralph had said. However, on my second night in the big leagues I got my first base hit, a ninth-inning single that helped beat Milwaukee again, 4–1. I reached base all five times I went to bat—and probably would have gotten a couple more hits if Gene Lamont, our catcher and the slowest runner on the team, hadn't been on base ahead of me each time. I kept hitting the ball on the ground, and the Brewers kept forcing Lamont at second base, so all I got were three fielder's choices. I scored one run and stole a couple of bases, and in the clubhouse I was told it had been a long while since a Tiger had stolen two bases in a single game. All of a sudden I felt pretty good about my big league career.

We flew to Detroit after the game, and the next afternoon we met the Baltimore Orioles at Tiger Stadium. It was the NBC-TV game of the week, and Tony Kubek had me and Baltimore pitcher Jim Palmer on his pre-game show. Standing on the sidelines while Kubek interviewed Palmer, I recalled what I had told the guys in the parole camp. I said I'd be in the major leagues and they'd be watching me on

TV in one year's time. And there I was. I could hardly believe it.

I was still in a daze, but I wasn't quite as nervous as I had been that first night in Milwaukee. My mother, my father, and a lot of friends were at the game, and more than anything I wanted to look good in front of them. When I ran out to center field at the start of the first inning I looked up into the bleachers and saw my brother Gerald sitting with a group of my friends. They were holding up a banner that said "LeFlore's East Side Legion." That made up for the names some of the other fans were calling me; it seemed as though nearly everyone else in the stands felt obliged to remind me that I had been in jail.

The best I could do in that game was an infield single in the eighth inning.

The next day we played a doubleheader with the Orioles, and in the first inning I walked, stole second, and scored on Al Kaline's sacrifice fly. I didn't look upon it as anything more than a run, but when I walked in the sixth inning the fans began to chant, "Go! Go! Go!" Standing on first base, I glanced toward the stands. It looked as though all 34,317 people in the ball park were yelling, "Go! Go! Go!" I could feel the adrenalin flow. Thereafter, I sensed the excitement build every time I came up to bat.

After the doubleheader the reporters crowded around my locker even though I had gone 0 for 6. None of them had seen the fans in Tiger Stadium turned on like that before. One reporter wrote, "LeFlore is the most exciting thing that has happened to this tired Tiger team in years." The Tigers were not known as a running, base-stealing ball club. The year before, veteran Tony Taylor had led the team in stolen bases with nine; in 1972 Taylor had been first with five. I had been in the big leagues only four days and already I had stolen three bases.

My biggest thrill that first year, aside from just being in the big leagues, was my first home run. It came on August 12, off Nelson Briles of Kansas City. He threw me a slider in the third inning, and I hit a line drive into the rightfield seats to help win the game for Mickey Lolich. It sent chills right through me. After I had rounded the bases and touched home plate I took my time walking back to the dugout. One reporter wrote that it took me longer to walk to the dugout than it did to trot around the bases. I was so excited I wanted to jump for joy, but I didn't want to act like a rookie, so I kept my head down and my feelings inside.

I had heard about rookies getting the silent treatment from their teammates when they hit their first home run—the guys would sit on the bench and pretend that nothing had happened—but I didn't get that kind of reception at all. Ralph Houk was first to greet me. "Good job, Ronnie," he said. Everybody shook my hand. They treated me as though I were one of the better ballplayers and acted as if they assumed I would be winning ball games for them.

Still I didn't really feel like part of the team. Al Kaline, Bill Freehan, Willie Horton, and Mickey Lolich had been together for a long time; they had been World Champions in 1968. I didn't think I belonged with players like that yet. I was only learning the game, and while I was sure I would be able to play with them some day I didn't think I was ready now. I was awed by my teammates.

Gates Brown was a big help during those first two months, introducing me to people around the league and showing me what was expected of a big league ballplayer. Gates had been in prison too, but I didn't look at him as another ex-con. All I thought about was baseball. Gates was a good hitter who had proven himself, and I figured he could help me become a good hitter. I think I may have listened to him a little more closely, though, because he had been in prison.

I always knew when I had done something wrong. When the team got back to the hotel after a game, Gates would say, "Let's go someplace."

In the minor leagues I had become a little lackadaisical. I could outrun everybody and I knew I was going to play every day no matter what, so I didn't always go all out. I got the idea I ought to pace myself, and this carried over when I went to the big leagues. But Gates kept after me.

We'd go for a few drinks and he'd say, "Look, man, this is no place to be bullshitting. You've got to give one hundred percent all the time. This game may look easy, but it's not. You've got to bust your ass at all times." Gates Brown had a big influence on my career: He made me hustle.

When the fans, especially in New York and Boston, called me Jailbird and names like that, I asked Gates how long it was going to continue.

"Look, man," he said. "I went through it—and times then were much harder than they are now. I made it. You can too."

Gates Brown was in the Ohio State Reformatory, serving two years for breaking and entering, when the Tigers found him in 1960. He went on to become the most prolific pinch-hitter the American League has ever seen.

"Ron's attitude wasn't the best when he first came up," recalls Brown, now a member of the Tiger

scouting staff. "*At times he didn't work as hard as he could, and I got on him a little bit.*

"*I told him, 'This is your last go-round, just like it was for me, and if you don't take advantage of it, you're never going to get another chance.' I suppose the fact that I was also an ex-con may have made him listen to me a little more than he ordinarily might have. All I did was tell him what I had been through.*

"*I warned him about associating with his old friends in Detroit. I knew they'd come after him, just like they used to come after me whenever I went back to Cleveland. I told him, 'You've got to make a choice: Do you want to be messing with them, or do you want to pursue a career?' "*

Jim Campbell and Hoot Evers both warned me that I would have to put up with a helluva lot of questions about my past, and I had been interviewed quite a bit in the minor leagues, so I pretty much knew what to expect. But, it was worse than they said it would be.

I got the same questions every day, day in and day out, wherever I went.

"Why were you in prison, Ronnie?"

"When did you start playing baseball?"

"You mean you didn't play any sports at all in school?"

It became monotonous after a while, and I got a little teed off. Sometimes the same reporter would come back two or three times and ask the same questions. One guy kept asking, "Do you think they brought you up too soon?"

Finally I said to him, "Look, I wasn't the one who decided I was to come up to the major leagues. That was up to the manager and the general manager. Why don't you ask them why I'm here?"

I tried to be cooperative, but soon I was dodging the press. If a writer called, I wouldn't call him back. I was afraid I would say something that would embarrass me. I was embarrassed enough by the fact I had been in prison, and I didn't want to say something that would make me look even worse.

Playing in my hometown didn't make matters easier. The Detroit newspapers, the *Free Press* and the *News,* paid more attention to me than they would have if I had been from California or New York. There was something about me in the papers almost every day. My old friends and people who knew my parents read the articles and called my mother's house constantly, asking for tickets.

I would promise to leave tickets and then forget about it because I had so many other things on my mind. I was worried about giving the right answers to reporters' questions; I was worried about playing baseball and afraid I might be sent back to the minor leagues; and I was worried about my parole and how much hassle I was going to have with my new parole officer in Detroit.

Sometimes I promised more tickets than I was allowed. Each player gets six tickets for each home game—four for his immediate family and two for friends—and I would get requests for ten or twelve tickets per game. I saw players going around the clubhouse before a game, asking if they could use their teammates' tickets that night, but I didn't think I had a right to do that.

I went back to the old neighborhood a few times to see my friends, but I avoided that environment as much as possible. I moved out of my mother's house and into an apartment so that no one could find me. Many of the guys I grew up with were in prison or were drug addicts. A lot of them were dead. My former best friend, Antoine, was shot and killed trying to rob a jewelry store in Mount Clemens, Michigan, in 1973.

I knew I couldn't associate with my old friends any more—particularly while I was on parole. But I was surprised at the reception I got the few times I did return. Drug addicts are looked on as the scum of the earth, people who will kill, steal, do anything to get drugs. But these guys weren't like that. Several old friends told me, "Look, man, don't come around here any more. You don't need this hassle. You don't want to be a part of what's going on here. You started out here, but there's no reason for you to mess up now. You got an opportunity, now do something with it."

That really surprised me. I never expected that kind of advice from addicts, not even those who were old friends. "Hey, man," I told them, "I can't ever forget you. You're part of me; you grew up with me." But I realized they were right, and I didn't go back.

After I had been with the Tigers for a couple of weeks we went on a week-long road trip to California. The first night in Oakland I was alone in the trainer's room before the game, trying to relax, when I noticed the box in which the players lock their valuables while they're on the field. I had seen the veteran players put big wads of money into the box before they dressed and I figured there had to be close to $10,000 there.

"Damn," I thought, "there's a nice little score there." I sat on the trainer's table, thinking how easy it would be to steal that money. But if I stole the money, I couldn't leave the ball club, or they'd know for sure it had been me. And

I wouldn't feel like hanging around with all that money, either.

Then I realized what I was doing. "You fool! What the hell are you thinking like that for anyway?" I asked myself. "You've got a chance to make much more money than that on your own. Are you going to blow it?" I felt ashamed of myself as I ran through the tunnel and out onto the field. That was the last time I thought of stealing anything—from anyone.

I got along well with most of my teammates, though I think a few of them resented the attention the press gave me. Willie Horton certainly didn't go out of his way to talk to me or make me feel at home, and he was the top black star on the team. It's understandable. I took a lot of the publicity away from him. He went from being kingfish to being goldfish, and I kept waiting for Willie to give me some encouragement. His roommate, Eddie Brinkman, talked to me all the time. He'd put his arm around me and say, "So you fucked up. Don't let it bother you. Everybody fucks up." But Willie just sat in his corner by himself, never saying a word to me. After a while I didn't care.

No one said anything to my face, but an incident in Anaheim, after a game in which Nolan Ryan of the California Angels struck me out four times, indicated how some of the Tigers felt. I was going into a hotel bar when I passed Woodie Fryman and Jim Ray, two pitchers the Tigers had gotten from the National League. "I guess he'll keep his mouth closed now," Fryman said loud enough for me to hear.

I thought Mickey Stanley and I might have harsh words when he came off the disabled list in September; I assumed he would have some ill-feeling toward me. Mickey had been an outstanding centerfielder for a long, long time, and I had walked in and taken over his job. But Mickey didn't say a word; he turned out to be one of the nicest guys on the team, and he taught me a lot about playing center field.

Other people helped, too. The first time I saw Maury Wills, the NBC television announcer who once held the record for stolen bases, I asked him for a few pointers. He took me to the rear of the clubhouse and gave me a couple of tips on how to get a better jump on the pitcher when I was on base. I stole a base that afternoon, and after the game Maury sent a note down to the clubhouse. "Great job!" it said. "You sure learn fast."

This is not to suggest I was a good base-stealer—or a good centerfielder or even a good major league ballplayer —in 1974. Time and time again I came racing in for a line drive only to see it sail over my head. I misjudged so many fly balls that I lost count, and several times I got caught looking around into the stands when the ball was hit. I had trouble with the strike zone and with curve balls; I was bailing out and striking out all the time. I didn't know the pitcher's moves. Most of the time I stole on sheer speed.

I didn't receive a great deal of instruction in the year I spent in the minor leagues. In Clinton the team was fighting for the pennant, so Jim Leyland didn't have time to teach. And since the Florida State League is considered the elite league in Class A baseball, everyone assumes that a guy knows how to play the game when he reaches that level. Most of what I knew about baseball I picked up on my own.

Every day my inexperience exhibited itself in a different way. A month after I joined the club Hal Middlesworth, the Tigers' public relations director, asked me to answer some questions on a personal information form for his files. It was easy.

"Did you ever play Little League baseball?" he asked.

"No."

"Did you ever play Babe Ruth League baseball?"

"No."

"Pony or Colt League baseball?"

"No."

"High School baseball?"

"No."

"College baseball?"

"No."

"American Legion baseball?"

"No."

"Sandlot baseball?"

"No."

That pretty well summed up my amateur baseball career.

I heard players talk about keeping "book" on pitchers and hitters, and I assumed they carried little books around in their pockets and wrote all that shit down. I didn't realize that you were supposed to keep it all upstairs, in your head. I didn't know how I was going to remember all the different pitchers and the different hitters.

In spite of my mistakes Ralph Houk kept me in the line-up, just as he had promised. He refused to let me be down on myself. Following a game in which I'd made a costly error or struck out in a crucial situation, I'd be sitting in the clubhouse with my head down after most of the other players had left, and Ralph would come by and say, "Don't worry about it, Ronnie. You still don't have a helluva lot of baseball experience. You'll improve."

He would always bring up Mickey Mantle as an example. He said Mantle had no idea of the strike zone when he first came up with the New York Yankees; he struck out regularly. Yet he became one of the great hitters of all time.

"Just go out there every day, believing, 'This son of a bitch can't strike me out,' " Ralph kept telling me. The trouble was, I knew the son of a bitch could.

I was so excited at being in the big leagues that I didn't have to run before a game to get my legs loose; the sensation of just being there seemed to loosen me up automatically. But I was jittery. At times, standing at the plate, I was shaking so much that there was no way in the world I could have gotten a base hit.

Deep down inside I knew I wasn't ready to play in the major leagues. I thought I had been brought up to boost attendance and take some of the heat off the manager and general manager because the team wasn't going anywhere except last place. In any business, if management can come up with a gimmick to attract interest, they'll use it. I was the Detroit Tigers' gimmick. I was a Detroit boy, I had been in prison, I was having a good year in the minor leagues, and I was more exciting than anyone else in their farm system. I was certain to create interest among the fans.

Sure I was being used. The fans expected too much of me as a result of the publicity I received, and they booed me because of it. But I wasn't going to tell the Tigers I didn't want the chance. I was going to have to learn to play major league baseball some day—and, I figured, the sooner the better. I made an ass of myself at times, but at times I made myself proud.

Tiger General Manager Jim Campbell vehemently denies that Ron was called up in 1974 to sell tickets or to divert the fans' attention from the fact that the team was headed for its first last-place finish in twenty-two years.

"Nothing is further from the truth," Campbell

*insists. "We had a lot of discussion about whether to
bring up Ron or Leon Roberts, another outfielder.
We thought Ron had so many tremendous pluses
going for him that he was ready to play in the major
leagues. In no way did we do it to sell tickets. Since
I've been associated with this ballclub we haven't
had to operate that way."*

At the end of the season I still didn't consider myself a
full-fledged major leaguer. Ralph Houk had said he'd be
happy if I hit .230 or even .220, and I had batted .260 my
first two months in the big leagues. In 59 games I had stolen
23 bases in 32 attempts—the most by any Tiger since Jake
Wood stole 24 in a full year twelve seasons earlier. I made
eleven errors, but six of those were on fly balls I overran. Yet
the moment I returned to the Florida Instructional League
that fall and was back among the guys I had played with in
Clinton and Lakeland, I felt like a minor leaguer again. It
wasn't until the following spring that it dawned on me: I was
a big league baseball player!

Number One Clown

I had the world by the tail. I was young, I was free, I had
plenty of money in my pocket, and wherever I went people
fawned over me and paid attention to everything I said. All
of a sudden I had everything going for me.

In January 1975 the Tigers invited me on their annual
midwinter publicity tour to show me off to the writers and
radio announcers in the little towns around the state. I was
a celebrity: I was their centerfielder. When the writers de-
scribed me as "the next Tiger superstar" the ball club did
nothing to discourage them. I was the symbol of the Tiger
youth movement, their hope for the future. Jim Campbell
gave me an $8,000 raise, and I knew there was more where
that came from.

On January 26, as I prepared to leave Detroit for spring
training, my parole was dropped. That was a load off my
mind! While you're on parole you're not supposed to associate with anyone carrying a concealed weapon (as if you

could tell who's carrying a concealed weapon), you're not to associate with drug addicts or dealers, you're not even to associate with other ex-cons. When I was released from Jackson just about everyone I knew fit into one of those categories. I could have been sent back to prison for violating my parole every time I stopped to say hello to someone.

From the moment training camp opened Ralph Houk made it clear that I was going to be the Tigers' full-time centerfielder no matter what Mickey Stanley did in spring training. I had it made.

Tiger owner John Fetzer offered to pay half the fee for any player who wanted to get involved in Transcendental Meditation, so I took the course and began meditating for twenty minutes, twice a day. This enabled me to relax, which was something I had been unable to do in 1974. I felt better during the day, and I was able to fall right asleep at night. Nothing could stop me now; I was looking forward to having a fantastic season.

When we met the St. Louis Cardinals in an exhibition game I cornered Lou Brock and asked for tips on stealing bases. After all, he was the best—and now I wanted to be.

Brock told me to study each pitcher until I discovered which part of his body moved first when he began his throw to the plate. It could be his head, his waist, or his shoulder. Brock said that once I learned that, all I had to do was to watch that one spot to know when to run.

I stole a base that very afternoon. Brock tried to steal one too, but he was thrown out. I was so proud! I was still patting myself on the back when I was picked off second with the bases loaded and Willie Horton waiting at the plate in the bottom of the ninth. I had seen Ted Simmons, the Cardinal catcher, give relief pitcher Elias Sosa the signal to throw to second base—but I didn't realize until later what the signal meant. I still had a lot to learn.

When the writers asked me what sort of season I expected to have in 1975, I predicted I'd steal between fifty and sixty bases and hit over .300. When one reporter pointed out that those statistics would add up to the best season by a Tiger player since Ty Cobb, I didn't bat an eye.

I was brimming with confidence; there was nothing I couldn't do. I assumed that since I had hit .339 in the minor leagues I could hit it in the majors too. After all, I had improved a great deal since Lakeland. There was not a pitcher in the league I thought I couldn't hit. If I hit over .300, it would be no problem stealing sixty bases because I'd be on base so much.

I didn't have an outstanding spring, but I could see tremendous improvement in myself. I batted .291 and stole twelve bases in fourteen attempts. While I still had trouble on fly balls directly over my head, I felt more comfortable and more sure of myself in center field.

The first half of the season reinforced my high opinion of myself. I made up for a lot of my earlier mistakes. The first time I faced Jim Slaton (who had made life so miserable for me that first night in Milwaukee) I collected two singles and a double. Slaton was impressed. I was elated.

I enjoyed such a good first half that I thought I might make the All-Star team. At the All-Star break I was batting .289 with 25 stolen bases and 28 runs batted in. I recalled my prediction of fifty or sixty stolen bases and a .300 batting average; at the halfway point I was right on schedule.

Everything seemed so easy. There was no way anyone could stop me from hitting the ball, getting on base, and stealing. I began taking my hits and stolen bases for granted.

I had such a big head I could hardly get my hat on.

Suddenly the hits stopped falling in and the opportunities to steal ceased to exist. At first I didn't realize what was happening. I had become lax at the plate; I underestimated my opponents; I was in a rut and I was digging myself in deeper.

I was pulling my head and lunging at the plate. I had lost my timing. I began pressing, trying to hit a home run every time. Instead of concentrating and trying to make contact with the ball I became overly aggressive. I would see the pitch coming, but because I was in such a hurry to get to the ball I would overswing. I tried to force myself to stay back and wait for the pitch, but I couldn't do it. Pitchers began fooling me with curve balls more and more. When I finally realized what was happening it was too late.

I was afraid of losing my job in center field. I was afraid of being sent to the minors. And the more I worried, the worse things got.

I couldn't eat, I couldn't sleep; I thought only about snapping out of that slump. I was always tense and I no longer bothered with Transcendental Meditation. I didn't think anything could help me. I began running around at night, drinking heavily, trying to relieve the pressure that had built up inside. Jim Campbell threatened to send me back to Evansville if I didn't settle down and straighten myself out.

It was like being trapped in a bad dream; it was the same feeling I had had when I first went to prison. My teammates tried to encourage me, but I was so down on myself that everything they said went in one ear and out the other. Whenever I went to the ball park I figured I would strike out two or three times. If we were facing a good pitcher, I knew I didn't stand a chance. I was beaten before the game began.

Because I was lunging at it, the ball kept hitting the bat near my right thumb, and my thumb became so badly bruised I could hardly swing. That made the situation even worse.

I was surprised that Ralph Houk kept me in center field. Every day I expected him to put Mickey Stanley out there. Anyone could have played the position better than I. Several times I went to Ralph and asked, "What am I doing wrong? Tell me what I should do to get out of this rut."

Each time he would say, "Hang in there, Ronnie. I told you it wasn't going to be easy. You're going to have to take things as they come and learn from your mistakes."

I tried, but every time I made a mistake I was down on myself more than ever. Guys offered me advice, but I wouldn't listen—I thought this was something I had to work out on my own. I thought about asking Ralph to take me out of the line-up because my head wasn't in the game, but I was afraid if I did that I'd never get back in.

Meanwhile the ball club was in the middle of a near-record 19-game losing streak that put us in the cellar of the American League East for the second year in a row. The Tigers were the laughing stock of baseball, and I was the number one clown.

During the first half of the season the press and public had been interested in my past because I was playing so well. During the second half the same people complained because the Tigers had brought me to the major leagues so soon.

I began to think that maybe they were right—maybe I didn't belong in the big leagues.

No longer did Ralph Houk compare Ron to superstars such as Mickey Mantle and Stan Musial. But he stuck with him, and he was criticized extensively as a result.

"Knowing the type of personality Ronnie has, I was afraid that if I took him out of the line-up, he would lose his confidence completely," Houk explains. "I didn't know if he'd ever bounce back.

"Ronnie is a pretty high-strung guy. He's different. If he had played a lot of baseball, I would have been able to talk to him in a way that he would have understood.

"Quite honestly, it reached a point where I didn't know if he would ever learn to play center field. I thought maybe we had made a mistake; I thought about moving him to right field where he wouldn't have so much ground to cover.

"Several times I figured I was going to have to take him out of the line-up even if it ruined him. Things were that bad. Then he would have a good game or make a good play, and I'd decide to stick with him a while longer. I kept telling myself he was bound to snap out of it sooner or later. The tools were always there; he has great natural ability. We had nowhere to go that year—we weren't going to win any pennants. I thought, 'If we're going to build a ballclub, we might as well find out how good this guy is going to be.'"

If I didn't have enough on my mind, there was an FBI agent waiting in Ralph's office when I got to the ball park one afternoon. He said he had heard my name mentioned in bookie joints around Detroit. He didn't accuse me of anything, but he gave me his card and told me to call him if anything happened he should know about.

I wasn't betting. My knowledge of betting was limited to what Jimmy the Greek said in the newspaper. I wasn't interested in that sort of thing; I had never been in a bookie joint, and I didn't even know what they looked like.

Though the agent told me not to worry, I wondered whether I had accidentally become involved with somebody like that. I began to imagine that the FBI was watching me all the time, and I told some of my friends not to come around any more. I was afraid they might be involved in some criminal activity and that, with the FBI watching me, I'd get caught in the middle. It frightened me so much I would just go to the ball park, play baseball, and return to my apartment. I was afraid to go anywhere else.

I was striking out so frequently that it became embarrassing. Instead of thinking about getting a base hit when I went to bat, all I could think about was not striking out. It got ridiculous near the end of the season: I was swinging at bad pitches and I wasn't even coming close. There were newspaper articles about my strikeouts nearly every day as I closed in on the all-time Tiger record for strikeouts. (The record is 141; I only missed it by two.)

I batted .206 after the All-Star break and stole only three bases in the final three months of the season. I realized I wasn't the best player in baseball or even in the American League. Until then I had believed I was—yes, I really did. Now I knew I didn't know as much about baseball as I thought I did.

I believe the Tigers expected too much of me in 1975. As a result I expected too much of myself. They knew how limited my experience was and how difficult the game is, even if I didn't. They set a helluva burden on my back, putting me in center field and having me lead off every day when I had been out of prison only a year.

They looked to me to be a leader on the team, and I didn't know how to handle it. I became cocky, predicting I was going to do this and that, because I assumed that was the way a leader was supposed to act. I was merely trying to protect myself; I didn't know what else to do in that situation.

When the season ended I took twelve days off, then began playing baseball for the Mayaguez Indians in the Puerto Rico League. Harvey Kuenn, who won the batting title with the Tigers in 1959 and is now a coach with the Milwaukee Brewers, was the manager at Mayaguez, and the Tigers sent me to him to learn to play baseball.

When I arrived I told Kuenn, "I made a lot of mistakes in the big leagues this year. My hitting wasn't nearly what it should be, and my fielding needs a lot of improvement. I hope you'll be able to help me."

"Ron, I watched you a lot," Kuenn said, "and you were pulling your head off the ball and trying to hit home runs. You're not a home run hitter. That was your big problem." I realized that he was right. After all I had been through in 1975, I still considered myself a home run hitter.

In practice the next day Kuenn called me aside and explained, "What I want you to do is to stand up at the plate, don't move your legs at all, just swing the bat with your arms, and concentrate on making contact with the ball."

For the next week, until the winter league season opened, I took an hour of extra batting practice every day, applying the advice Harvey had given me. I tried to hit every ball where it was pitched without moving my feet. If the ball was outside, I reached for it; if it was inside, I fought the ball off and pushed it to right field. I found I could hit like that—or at least I could make contact. My confidence began coming back.

Jim Campbell was in Puerto Rico for a general managers' meeting and came to see me play the opening game. I started off with a bang: I got a couple of hits, stole a couple of bases, and scored the winning run.

Kuenn reminded me every day to stay back and concentrate on making contact with the ball. After a while it began to feel natural; I couldn't have lunged at the ball if I wanted to. I discovered that I could see the ball better, and I could usually hit it if I waited for the pitch.

My fielding also improved. In 56 games I made only thirteen errors—and they weren't the stupid mistakes I had been making in the major leagues. I learned to throw the ball to the proper base and to get back in position to catch the ball instead of trying to outrun everything that was hit my way. That was one thing I picked up by myself; I realized one day that it made more sense.

I was able to relax in Puerto Rico. The press wasn't hounding me constantly, as they had been doing in the major leagues. I had time to think about what I should be doing. I had a room on the ocean, and many nights I sat on the beach counting waves or counting stars, thinking about the things I had to do if I wanted to continue to be a major league ballplayer. Right there in Puerto Rico I told myself I was going to have a fantastic season in 1976.

The Urge to Kill

I couldn't wait for spring training to begin. Unfortunately, the owners and Marvin Miller, the leader of the players' union, didn't share my enthusiasm. Negotiations on a new basic contract bogged down, and the owners—including John Fetzer of the Tigers—locked the players out of training camp. We weren't allowed to use the equipment or the facilities at Marchant Stadium; we weren't even allowed in our own clubhouse.

Several Tigers who felt the way I did showed up in Lakeland in the middle of February anyway. We were ballplayers, not labor negotiators. John Hiller, our lefthanded relief ace, who had been in Florida on his own for more than a month recovering from a sore arm, took charge and arranged an informal training camp for those who were interested. Hiller obtained permission to use Henley Field, the ball park where the Tigers had trained until Marchant Stadium was built in 1966. He snuck into Marchant one morning and "borrowed" bats and a couple of boxes of balls, and held our own spring training while Miller and the owners argued.

It wasn't the same, but it was better than nothing. At least we were able to get our legs in shape and take batting practice. Since we weren't allowed to wear our uniforms, the guys worked out in whatever clothes they had. Some wore sweat suits, some wore levis, some wore gym shorts; we were quite a sight. There were about a dozen players in the Lakeland area, although they didn't all show up every day. Hiller himself took a few days off to go fishing. Ralph Houk and Jim Campbell weren't allowed on the field, so there was no one to take attendance. Willie Horton wanted to join us, but Hiller chased him away. He was afraid that Willie, with his power, would hit all our balls over the fence. Then where would we be?

The Tigers refused to pay our room and board until spring training opened officially, so I moved in with a girl I had met the year before. It wasn't the best arrangement— she already had a roommate—but at least the price was right.

As the debate between Miller and the owners dragged on into March, Horton and some of the others talked about going home. We all realized we weren't accomplishing a lot in our makeshift practice sessions, and some guys were running short of money. I was determined to stay in Lakeland even if I had to get a part-time job. I was certain things would be settled eventually and I wanted to be ready to play baseball when camp opened. In 1975 I had learned how hard it is to play baseball; I realized how much study, how much hard work, how much devotion you have to give to the game. I knew what to expect now, what I could do, and how well prepared I would have to be in the future. The nightmare I went through during the second half of the 1975 season had matured me—in more ways than one.

Back in Detroit Ron Ishoy, a reporter for the *Free Press*, wrote an article that said I was actually four years older than I led people to believe. Suddenly I was the center of controversy again.

I lied about my age when I first signed with the Tigers in 1973; I admit that. In prison Jimmy Karalla had advised me to knock a couple of years off my age. He said that if the Tigers thought I was twenty-one rather than twenty-three, I might stand a better chance of making it to the major leagues. So, when the Tigers asked me to fill out a questionnaire, I put my birthdate down as June 16, 1952, instead of 1950. I was afraid that if they knew my real age, they'd think I was too old to begin a professional baseball career.

Jim Campbell had a copy of my parole report that gave my actual date of birth, and he asked me which date was correct. I chose the lesser age. At that point I was happy to have a chance to play pro ball; I think anyone with my background who suddenly had a chance to become a respectable citizen would have done the same thing. I didn't see myself as doing something wrong; I was only anxious to take advantage of an opportunity to better myself.

When everyone seemed to accept the younger age, I assumed I didn't have to worry about it any more. I don't know what brought about the article in the *Free Press*. I never met the reporter, and I don't know where he got the idea that I was born in 1948. But I felt picked on because I was an ex-con. I'm sure other players have lied about their age without a big deal being made of it, and I resented the fact that so much fuss was made over my doing it.

> *The Tigers, who apparently realized what Ron was doing and officially sanctioned his effort in the club press guide, claimed that Ron's actual age was of little consequence.*
>
> *"One or two years—who the hell cares?" manager Ralph Houk asked. "I don't give a damn if he's 58, as long as he can run and hit and throw. I don't think anybody sitting in the stands cares how old a guy is, so long as he's doing the job."*
>
> *General Manager Jim Campbell cited former pitcher Satchel Paige, whose actual age is still a mystery, and Billy Bruton, who admittedly aged four years the day he retired from the Tigers.*
>
> *"We never denied there was a discrepancy about LeFlore's age," Campbell pointed out. "But it was no big deal. Even if we go by the highest age we have for him in our files, he's still a relatively young man.*
>
> *"I'm disappointed that some people feel they have to undress the kid like that. He paid his penalty and he's trying for a fresh start in life. I don't think it's fair."*

My past was being plastered all over the newspapers again. The reporter even brought up my juvenile arrest record and claimed I had been less than honest about my criminal activities.

I never denied that I had been in trouble before I went to prison. But I certainly didn't go around bragging about how bad I was. I tried to explain my childhood to anyone who asked, and I didn't have to be as open about it as I was. I don't think most people would have been as free with their comments as I was, but I wanted those questions out of the way once and for all.

In 1976 I thought all that was behind me. I figured the press would want to talk about my career, and I'd be able to concentrate on baseball. I found out I was wrong. Questions about my actual age kept popping up after the owners reached agreement with the players association and the training camps finally opened on March 18.

The day after we began practicing, Ralph Houk was quoted as saying that Mickey Stanley and I were going to be fighting for the centerfield job. That tightened me up even more. I had come to spring training determined to show everyone how much I had improved in Puerto Rico. I felt that in spite of the horseshit season I had had in 1975, I deserved to be the Tigers' starting centerfielder in 1976.

When I read what Ralph had said my attitude changed. I began pressing, trying too hard to look good. I got into the habit of lunging at the ball again, and I started striking out. Yet I still thought I deserved to open the regular season; mentally and physically, I was ready.

When we arrived in Cleveland for the April 10 opener, Ralph announced that Ben Oglivie would be the starting centerfielder. I was crushed. I realized I hadn't had a good spring, and I knew Mickey Stanley was an outstanding centerfielder, but when I saw Oglivie's name in the line-up I didn't know what to think. I saw myself sitting on the bench or being sent to the minor leagues; I imagined all sorts of horrible things happening to me.

The more I thought about it, the madder I got. I didn't have a good year in 1975, but half the centerfielders in the league had had lower batting averages than my .258. I didn't have a good second half, but the entire team had had a bad second half. We lost 102 games in 1975, and I didn't lose all 102 of them.

If I'm not going to start, I told myself, there's no sense in working hard. I quit running in the outfield, I quit exercising, I quit everything. I was so mad at Ralph I wouldn't talk to him.

The season was a week old before I finally got into a game. In the eighth inning against the California Angels in Anaheim, Ralph sent me in to pinch-run for Gary Sutherland. I stole second base and scored on Willie Horton's double as we rallied for three runs to take the lead. But in the bottom of the eighth Ralph sent Mickey Stanley out to play centerfield—for defensive purposes. That really pissed me off.

I made my first start the next afternoon, and I got a hit. But when I got to the ball park the following day I looked at the line-up card and saw that Mickey Stanley was playing center field.

I wondered what was going on. I asked the writers traveling with the Tigers if Ralph had given them any indication why I wasn't playing. They said they thought it was only a temporary situation.

I made up my mind I was going to show Ralph—and everyone else—that I could play baseball. I realized that I was only hurting myself with my bad attitude. I began running again, getting myself back into shape so that when I did get a chance to play I'd be ready. I was more determined now than I had ever been about anything in my life.

Although Ralph Houk told the press that Ben Oglivie had opened the season in order to have another lefthanded bat in the Tiger line-up, he admits he was also anxious to let LeFlore know he didn't have things made.

"It wasn't that I had any doubt that Ronnie would eventually be our regular centerfielder, but I felt it would do him good to know the job wasn't completely his," Houk says. *"I wanted to make him realize there were other things he had to work on if he was ever going to be the player he could be. And I think it may have helped."*

I played the two remaining games in Oakland and was beginning to feel that center field was mine again. We returned to Detroit on April 23 to play the Texas Rangers, and I was on the field taking batting practice at about eleven when Mario, the clubhouse boy, told me there had been an emergency and I was to call home.

I phoned my girl friend, Deborah Hutchins, and asked her what was wrong. She wouldn't say anything and then started crying. Finally she sobbed, "I'm not supposed to tell you this, but I've got to; I can't keep it to myself any longer. Your brother Gerald was killed."

My heart stopped for a second. I felt as though a big blanket had been thrown over my head. I was sick to my stomach.

Deborah started to sob again. "Your mother told me not to tell you, but I thought you ought to know."

I hung up and then called my mother. I had to find out if it was true.

"Yes," she said, "Gerald is dead."

Unlike Deborah, my mother wasn't crying. I guess she was all cried out by then. I had stopped by her house that morning on my way to the ball park, and she hadn't said a word about it. But she already knew. She was all dressed up, and I assumed she had been to the store or out for a walk;

in fact she had just returned from the morgue.

"Do you want me to come home?" I asked.

"No," she said softly, "there's nothing you can do now. Stay at the ball park and try to play as best you can."

I hung up and sat alone in the little room in our clubhouse where the telephone is located. Gerald dead. It took a while for the shock to hit me. I didn't want to talk to anyone; there were no words that wanted to come out.

When I finally stood up my legs were shaking and I felt weak all over.

Ralph had already made out a new line-up with Mickey Stanley in center field, but I told him I would play. On the field all I could think about was my brother. I remembered how he used to tease me, always trying to aggravate me, when we were kids. We were always arguing or fighting about something—but I loved him.

During the game some fans in the centerfield bleachers kept booing me. "How old are you really, LeFlore?" they hollered. "Go back to jail, you can't play baseball!" I felt the urge to climb into the stands and kill someone.

Of course they had no idea my brother had just been killed. I doubt whether any one of them would have had the courage to go to work a few hours after learning that a brother had been killed. Every time I looked up into the bleachers I remembered the first game I had played in Tiger Stadium—when my brother and some friends had sat with the banner that said "LeFlore's East Side Legion."

I don't know how I played that day. I don't know how I was able to hold back the tears. I ached all over. My body felt so heavy, so tired. I couldn't concentrate on the game; his death was on my mind every pitch. Every time I stepped out of the batter's box I thought about my brother. I told myself I was playing the game in his memory. Somehow I got three hits.

> *The newspaper report of Gerald LeFlore's death was succinct and to the point: "The younger brother of Detroit Tiger centerfielder Ron LeFlore was shot to death early Friday during an argument with several men at an east side Detroit home."*
>
> *According to police, he was killed with a .30 caliber carbine at 2 A.M. Six men who were in the house at the time of the shooting were held for questioning, but no charges were ever filed. Witnesses said Gerald tried to shoot one of the other men with the gun and was accidentally shot in the struggle that ensued. An autopsy revealed codeine, morphine, and traces of methadone in LeFlore's body.*

I knew Gerald had had a problem with drugs. While I was in prison my mother petitioned the court and had him sent to the federal hospital in Lexington, Kentucky, for help. I thought he had kicked the habit, but when I got out of prison I discovered that he was messing with drugs again.

I talked to him and promised to help him as soon as I started making some money. I tried to convince him to continue his education. Gerald was very intelligent; when we were kids he always wanted to stay in the house and read books and study. I called him a sissy, but I was envious that he could read books I couldn't read even though he was a couple of years younger than me. While I was on the street stealing, he was in the house studying. At one time he was going to be a chemist; he even went to college for a while.

Then he began associating with the same kind of people

I had hung around with before I went to prison. Maybe he patterned himself after me, I don't know; I certainly hope not.

In 1975 one of his friends even kidnapped him and tried to get some ransom money from me, but Gerald got away from him. I tried to tell him that those people were no good, but he was headstrong and wouldn't listen. Gerald always thought he knew more than anyone else. Maybe he was too smart—or maybe he wasn't as smart as he thought he was.

On the day of his funeral I was completely out of it. I didn't know whether I was going or coming. I remember I cried a couple of times, but that's about all I remember. I know people kept coming up to me to say how sorry they were and things like that, but I don't remember who they were or what they said. I kept thinking only that my brother Gerald was dead.

The old Ron LeFlore definitely would have tried to get even with whoever had killed his brother, but I was past that point. I do think the police were a little negligent in handling the case; I'm sure the guys who were with my brother when he was killed were guilty of a felony, but the police accepted their story that it was an accident. I know my brother had drugs in his body, but that's beside the point. How can a person get shot in the chest with a high-power rifle when he's pointing that rifle at someone else? It doesn't make sense. Someday I would like to have the case reopened; I'd like to find out what really happened.

I owned the longest hitting streak in the major leagues, and nobody knew it. The press talked only about my age, my brother's death, and the fact that I had opened the season on the bench. Here it was May, I had collected at least one base hit in every game in which I had played, and whenever the reporters wanted to talk baseball they went to Willie Horton or Jason Thompson or Rusty Staub.

That was fine with me; I was satisfied to be a "sleeper." I didn't care whether I received a lot of attention or not— so long as people noticed me at the end of the year. Then I wanted them to say, "Hey, he had a helluva year."

I made up my mind I would keep my mouth shut and not try to predict what I was going to do. In 1975 I counted my games before they were played and my at-bats before they came. In 1976 I was determined to take my at-bats as my name was called. I was still confident, but it was a quiet and sure kind of confidence rather than the cocky confidence I had had the year before.

I cut down on my jiving in the clubhouse, too; I made up my mind to be more serious about the game. I was still making mistakes in the outfield, but they weren't as obvious as before. And I wasn't chasing bad pitches and making a fool of myself at the plate. As a matter of fact, I was playing pretty well.

Deborah Hutchins and I were living together, and on May 1, one week after my brother was killed, our daughter, LaRonda, was born. We were playing in Chicago when I got the call, and I was overjoyed. I had lost one love—my brother—but gained another. That afternoon I got two singles, scored two runs, and stole four bases as we trounced the White Sox, 9–1.

I was one short of the all-time Tiger record of five stolen bases in one game (set by Johnny Neun in 1927). Even Ty Cobb, great as he was, never stole more than four bases in one game in his career.

I was playing every day now, and I was hitting every time I played. My batting average climbed steadily toward .400 as my streak continued. I still hadn't been shut out.

One hit in particular gave me a big boost. In a game with Boston on May 17 I was hitless going into the bottom of the eighth. Luis Tiant was pitching for the Red Sox, and I realized it would most likely be my last turn at bat. Tiant got two quick strikes on me—the old Ron LeFlore would have given up right there, especially against a pitcher as good as Tiant—but I hung in there, telling myself he wouldn't get me out. Tiant threw me a slider, and I singled to left field. I had not only kept my streak alive, I showed I had improved as a hitter—period.

It didn't seem to matter what I did at the plate; everything was *right*. I knew, every day, every game, I was going to get another hit. That's the kind of confidence the hitting streak gave me.

Though I realized what was happening, I didn't begin thinking about my streak and keeping count until May 21, when I broke Al Kaline's modern Tiger record of twenty-two consecutive games with a first-inning single off Baltimore's Jim Palmer. Two days later I got four hits off Ken Holtzman and Dyar Miller of Baltimore to raise my average to .409. The press finally noticed my streak, and my teammates kidded me about breaking Joe DiMaggio's record of fifty-six consecutive games. Almost overnight the pressure began to build again.

When the team returned home the writers and radio announcers who had ignored me throughout the first two months of the season crowded around.

"How do you feel?"

"Has the pressure gotten to you yet?"

"Do you think you can break DiMaggio's record?"

"How long do you think your hitting streak will last?"

I enjoyed the attention at first, but before long the hitting streak was all I heard no matter where I went or what I did. I tried not to think about it, but the whole town was talking about my streak.

The pressure became almost unbearable. I had received a lot of publicity when I came up in 1974, but this wasn't the same. In 1974 I was in a daze; in 1976 I knew exactly what was happening. I had never been under that kind of pressure before, and I didn't know how to handle it.

I stopped reading the newspapers because I knew what would be in them. It didn't seem to matter to the press whether the Tigers won or lost; they were concerned only with whether or not I got another hit. I refused to listen to the radio. But I couldn't hide; every time I managed to put the streak out of my mind for a minute somebody would remind me of it.

At Tiger Stadium, when I ran out to my position after getting a hit, the fans in the centerfield bleachers would stand and cheer. I had lost some love for the fans in Detroit, but as they cheered me during my hitting streak my feelings toward them changed again. It was a complete turnabout: Everyone seemed to be behind me now. I began talking to the fans in the bleachers again, yelling to them between outs, sometimes even between pitches. Baseball became fun once more.

"LeFlore! LeFlore! LeFlore!" they chanted when I stretched my streak to twenty-nine games with a single and a home run in a doubleheader with Baltimore. That sounded so much better than Jailbird!

I got a triple my first time up on the following night off Baltimore's Ken Holtzman to make it thirty in a row. But on May 28 Ed Figueroa and Tippy Martinez of the New York Yankees combined to shut me out in four trips to the plate. In the first inning Figueroa jammed me with a curve ball, and I flied to Oscar Gamble in shallow right field. Again I felt the pressure increase.

When I stepped to the plate in the third inning, with rookie Jerry Manuel on second, I could hear the rhythmic clapping of the fans. I was tense; although I had insisted all along that it didn't mean that much to me, I didn't want my streak to end. With the count full at 3 and 2, I bounced another inside curve down the third base line. Graig Nettles, the Yankee third baseman, thought Manuel might try to steal on the play and was breaking toward the bag—which put him in perfect position to field the ball and throw me out. Had Nettles been in his regular position, well off the line, the ball might have bounced by him, or I might have been able to beat out a hit.

Manuel was on base again when I got up in the sixth inning, and again he may have played a role in my downfall. I grounded meekly to Yankee shortstop Jim Mason, who easily forced Jerry at second base. If Mason had been required to field the slow grounder and throw to first, I might have made it with my speed.

In the eighth inning I was desperate. I knew it was my last chance. In three earlier games I had kept my streak alive with a base hit in my final at-bat, and now I could sense the fans waiting and hoping for it to happen again.

I swung and missed at Tippy Martinez's first pitch. My heart was pounding. Chris Chambliss, the Yankee first baseman, was playing me deep, so I decided to surprise him with a bunt. But I fouled the pitch off and I was 0 and 2.

The Yankee catcher, Thurman Munson, went to the mound to talk to Martinez. Before the game he had boasted to the writers that the Yankees were going to stop my streak. As I watched him walk back from the mound, I wanted very much to make a liar out of him.

Munson called for a fastball. I'll give him credit for that; at least he didn't try to make me chase another curve. The pitch was down and in—too far down and too far in, I thought. I watched it go by and then watched plate umpire Jerry Neudecker raise his right fist high in air. "Strike Three!" he bellowed.

My last chance to get a hit was gone. He hadn't even given me the benefit of the doubt.

The fans were chanting "LeFlore! LeFlore! LeFlore!" as I returned to center field in the top half of the ninth, but it wasn't the same. I waved my cap a couple of times, but I could feel the adrenalin that had built up rushing out of my body. I suddenly felt very, very relaxed; I was more relieved than disappointed. It was over.

Over, but not soon forgotten. For his efforts Ron LeFlore was voted Player of the Month of May in the American League (in the wake of his earlier honor as Player of the Week).

His hitting streak, from April 17 through May 27, had matched the longest by a Tiger since 1930. It was the second longest by any batter at the beginning of a season in baseball history. Only George Sisler of the St. Louis Browns got off to a better start, hitting safely in thirty-four consecutive games in 1925. It was the longest in the American League since Joe DiMaggio's brother Dom put together a thirty-four game streak with the Boston Red Sox in 1949. Since 1900 only twelve major leaguers enjoyed streaks that were longer.

Babe Ruth never had a thirty-game hitting streak. Neither did Lou Gehrig—or Ted Williams, Al Kaline, Mickey Mantle, or Hank Aaron. Baseball's Hall of Fame is filled with hitters—good hitters, great hitters—who never came close to doing what Ron LeFlore did in the first two months of 1976.

A Detroit mathematician computed the odds against a .258 hitter such as Ron opening the season with a thirty-game hitting streak at 65,500-to-1.

I was aware of the national publicity I had received because of my hitting streak, and I began to think about the

All-Star Game. I knew that many of the fans across the country based their votes on what they read in the newspapers or heard on TV. A lot of players don't care about the All-Star Game; they prefer to take the three days off. But I couldn't wait for the ballots to come in to find out how I was doing.

The All-Star Game had been a goal of mine since spring training. In fact I started thinking about it in Puerto Rico, when I lay under the stars trying to rebuild my confidence. I kept telling myself, You can make it! So long as I kept hitting, I figured I had a good chance.

I had watched my first All-Star Game on television in prison in 1971, and when I started playing pro ball I dreamed of playing in one some day. For me the All-Star Game was the ultimate—like playing in the World Series.

I would have been satisfied just to have made the team; getting elected to the starting line-up was a bigger thrill than being released from prison. I couldn't believe that 1,911,355 people had voted for me! Obviously the people in Detroit and throughout the United States realized I could play baseball and were willing to forget about my past.

I took my mother and father to Philadelphia for the game—we were all looking forward to seeing the sights—and I was in a daze once again. Then Darrell Johnson of Boston, the manager of the American League team, announced his starting line-up, and my heart sank. I would have to play left field to make room for Fred Lynn of the Red Sox, the only outfielder who had received more votes than I. I felt sick.

Left field was my position when I went to the minor leagues, but I hadn't played there since the middle of 1974. I had become so accustomed to center field that I had forgotten how to play left.

The day before the game Darrell hit fly balls to me in left field for about thirty-five minutes during practice. I began to feel more relaxed, but I still had no idea how I would react to balls hit to me during the game. I was frightened; I didn't want to make a mistake in my first All-Star Game.

Before the game President Ford came through the clubhouse and shook hands with the players. That was a thrill. When I was growing up I didn't even know who the President of the United States was.

Mark Fidrych, the Tigers' famous "Bird" and the American League's starting pitcher in the game, was sitting next to me when a couple of secret service agents approached him to ask if he'd like to present an autographed ball to the President. At first the Bird ignored the request.

"I've got a game to pitch," he said.

I almost fell off my stool. The secret service men laughed too, and later the Bird did give President Ford a ball.

Fortunately I didn't mess up during the game, although Greg Luzinski of Philadelphia hit a drive that almost got by me. My first time up I singled to left field off San Diego's Randy Jones, considered by many to be the best pitcher in baseball at that time. I should have gotten a hit my second time up, too, but I waited too long on the pitch because I knew Jones didn't throw very hard. I think that was why Darrell Johnson pulled me out of the game in the fifth inning. If I had gotten another hit, we might have scored—and the American League might have won an All-Star Game for a change.

I had hoped to play the entire game, but I wasn't disappointed about coming out. The big thing was just being there. I got to meet a number of top players from the National League and influential people from the business world. Most important, I played well and didn't embarrass myself. The world had seen that Ron LeFlore could play baseball.

That year was the Year of the Bird in Detroit. After the All-Star Game the season belonged to Mark Fidrych. Just playing on the same team with him was a trip. He's so flaky and so funny that he kept everyone on the team loose, along with himself. There's nothing phony about the Bird; he truly is crazy. The things he does—talking to the ball and wearing the same grubby clothes day after day—that's really him. He's a great guy; I love him!

The fans loved him, too. Everywhere we went they turned out in record numbers. Tiger Stadium was never so full as when he pitched. The response I got during my hitting streak was nothing compared to the treatment the Bird received.

The press swarmed around him wherever we played, and everything the Bird said in 1976 made headlines—even though it usually didn't make sense. That took a lot of pressure off the rest of the team, and we were able to concentrate on baseball. It's nice to get a lot of publicity, but it's nice not to have the writers and radio announcers following you around all the time, too.

I had an outstanding year in 1976—if I do say so myself. I cut down on strikeouts, I stopped chasing bad pitches, I turned the right way in the outfield even on balls hit over my head, and I ran the bases the way I always knew I could. Many said I was the most improved player in the American League in 1976, and I was inclined to agree. Aside from our fifth-place finish, the only thing wrong with 1976 was the fact that the season ended three weeks early for me.

We had to play a Sunday doubleheader in New York on September 12, and I got permission from Ralph Houk to skip batting practice and show up at the ball park an hour later than the rest of the team. Late in the season, if you've been playing every day, batting practice doesn't do you any good —especially when you're hitting .317.

I left a wake-up call for 11 A.M.; that would get me to Yankee Stadium in plenty of time for the one o'clock game. But the operator at the Roosevelt Hotel neglected to call. My phone finally woke me at 12:25 P.M.; it was the club-house man at Yankee Stadium calling to find out where I was. I jumped out of bed, pulled on my clothes, and brushed my hair while riding down in the elevator. I climbed in a cab and told the driver I'd give him an extra five bucks if he got me to the ball park in time for the game. He made it too, even though the Yankees were giving away free jackets to the kids that Sunday and the doubleheader had attracted a sell-out crowd. When we got caught in the traffic jam around Yankee Stadium the cabbie drove right up on the sidewalk.

It was ten minutes to one when I dashed into the club-house out of breath and began to dress. Most of the guys were already on the field, but the National Anthem hadn't been played yet, so I figured I could still make it. However, Ralph Houk sent Rusty Staub to tell me there was no need to hurry; he had scratched my name from the starting line-up.

I knew Ralph was pissed; during the game he kept giving me nasty looks. I didn't know what to say—I didn't have a good excuse—so I tried to act interested in the game and to cheer the other guys on. The Bird was going for his sixteenth win, and I was afraid that if we lost the game, my teammates would feel I had let them down. Fortunately we won, 6–0, and Ralph told me to get ready to start the second game. Houk said Jim Campbell, who was with us on the road trip, wanted to fine me, but he said he would try to talk him out of it.

Between games I loosened up as I always do by running sprints in the outfield. I grounded out leading off the top half of the first inning, and in the bottom half I took my place in center field. I felt better already.

The second Yankee hitter, former Tiger Elliott Maddox, hit a sinking line drive to left center field, and I charged the ball, trying to catch it on one hop. The outfield in Yankee Stadium was uneven—there was a little valley between center field and left field—and when I tried to plant my right foot to jump for the ball (which had taken a bad bounce) my knee locked. I felt something pop.

As soon as my feet left the ground I knew I had injured something. My right leg went limp, and there was no drive to my leap at all. Instead of coming down on my feet I threw my legs up in the air and landed on my back so I wouldn't make matters worse. I couldn't feel any pain, but I knew something was wrong.

They carried me off the field on a stretcher. Lying on the trainer's table in the clubhouse, I could see the edge of my kneecap pushing the skin up in the air. I thought I had broken my kneecap.

I touched my knee with my finger, and my finger sunk down into the socket, all the way to the second joint. "Oh, fuck!" I shouted, bringing trainer Bill Behm running in from the other room where he had been calling for a doctor. I was sure my career was over right there.

When I got to Lenox Hill Hospital the doctor told me

not to worry. I had ruptured the patella tendon, which held my right kneecap in place; the injury was serious but not the sort of thing that could end my career. They put my leg in a cast from ankle to thigh to hold the knee in place, and Vince Desmond, our traveling secretary, took me back to the hotel to pack my things. I flew back to Detroit and the next morning I underwent surgery at Henry Ford Hospital.

After a week in the hospital and six weeks in a cast I began a rehabilitation program to rebuild my leg. Dick Vitale, basketball coach at the University of Detroit, offered me the use of their facilities, and the school's trainer, Jack Moores, went right to work on me.

On the first day I could barely bend my knee, but after months of exercise and many hours in an ice-cold whirlpool I was one hundred percent recovered. All I had left to show for the accident was a huge scar on my knee in the shape of a question mark.

There was no question about my future. With the help of my agent, Bob Woolf of Boston, I signed a three-year, six-figure contract that will take me through 1979.

I first met Bob in 1974 when we were playing in Boston. Tiger radio announcer Ernie Harwell knew him and got the two of us together. I didn't feel then that I needed an agent (I had just started playing), but in 1975 Bob and I got closer and closer. He invited me to his home while the Tigers were in Boston; I ate with his family, I played pool with them in the basement, and they all seemed to be in my corner.

Bob told me he saw a great future for me, and I saw no reason why I shouldn't let him represent me. He talked to Jim Campbell and got me a nice raise in 1976. He now handles all my affairs and has my power of attorney. My paycheck from the Tigers goes to him every two weeks, and he gives me an allowance of $250 a week and takes care of my taxes and my bills. I like it that way; I don't have to worry about some bill collector banging on my door because I forgot to pay something when the team was out of town.

The guy has really been good to me. Whenever I need something or want something taken care of, it always seems as though it's done the next day. I take Bob's advice on a lot of things; he is truly looking out for my interests.

I had told myself before the 1976 season began that if I had a good year I was going to demand a long-term contract. I wanted some security. Although my statistics weren't as impressive as they might have been if I hadn't gotten hurt, I did bat .316 (the fifth best average in the American League) and I stole fifty-eight bases, the most by any Tiger since Ty Cobb stole sixty-eight in 1916.

I considered refusing to sign a contract and playing out my option, as Reggie Jackson and several others did in 1976. If the Tigers hadn't given me a decent long-term contract, I would have. I'm sure I could have gotten more money from another ball club as a free agent. But Detroit gave me the opportunity to better myself, and I owed them something for that. I owed them a lot.

An Altogether Different Life

16

I've been through hell in my life—on the streets, in prison, even playing baseball. I don't think there's a player in the game who has been through as much as I have, and I'm proud of that.

I'm proud of who I am and what I've accomplished. I won't say I'm proud of my past, but I'm not ashamed of it, either. I can't apologize for an altogether different life.

I feel as though I've been reincarnated, as though I lived one life before and I'm living a completely different life now. It's as if I had been born in one world, died, and came back in another that was one hundred percent the opposite. I can't believe how my life has changed since I began playing baseball.

I'm not a churchgoer, but I do believe in a Supreme Being, and I'm convinced that all this was in the plan for me when I was born. It had to be destined—how else can you explain it? How often does a major league manager go into

169

a prison? How often does a convict who has never played baseball get a chance to play pro ball? This had to be God's will.

What if Leroy hadn't testified against me and I had been set free rather than sent to Jackson? What if I had never met Jimmy Karalla? What if Billy Martin hadn't visited the prison? What if Mickey Stanley hadn't broken his hand?

People remark that I smile a lot. Well, I think I've got a lot to smile about. Baseball means the world to me. It's my chance to make a legitimate living; it helps me respect who and what I am; it's my means of washing my past out of everyone's mind.

Jim Campbell has been like a second father to me. I've spent hours in his office bullshitting about anything and everything. He gets pissed at me when I criticize the ball club, but he doesn't stay pissed very long.

I realize now that Ralph Houk was the major reason I got to the big leagues in the first place. He stuck his neck out for me; he put me in center field and left me there to learn, even though I obviously wasn't ready to play in the big leagues. He's one of the most inspiring persons I've ever met. His door is always open, and he never gets down on his players for their mistakes. The majority of the time he never says a word.

I still don't know a fourth of what I need to know to play in the major leagues. But my desire and determination are greater than my lack of experience. I have a lot of natural ability, that's true, but I think my desire is what keeps me in the game.

I enjoy everything that goes with being a ballplayer. I enjoy the applause from the fans, I enjoy the attention from the press, and I enjoy the girls a guy can get on the road just because he is a ballplayer.

I don't go overboard the way some players do, but there are girls I can get in touch with in just about every town in the American League. If I feel like messing around, I do; if I don't, I don't.

I've tried to stay cool. I've tried not to become big-headed just because I'm a ballplayer. I've tried to treat baseball as a job just like any other job.

I don't have any close friends among the Tigers. I hang around with a number of guys, but I prefer to be by myself a lot too. In 1976 Alex Johnson nicknamed me Trackdown because he and Willie Horton never saw me around the hotel on the road. They believed I was out tracking down women all the time.

If my baseball career ended tomorrow, I'm sure I wouldn't fall back into a life of crime. I know now that there are other ways, better ways, that I can make a living and survive.

I'm still tempted to smoke a little grass to relax or to be sociable with friends, but I haven't thought about hard drugs since I was in prison. Nothing could make me revert to my old ways.

I never go back to the old neighborhood any more. I may drive through it on the way to my mother's house, but that's it. Frankly, I'd be afraid to go there—it's gotten that bad. Things are much more desperate now than they were when I was growing up. There are more gangs, more drugs, more killings; most of the buildings are boarded up or burned out. It's desolate during the day and deadly at night.

I've gone back to Jackson Prison to visit several times since I was paroled. In fact, after my first season in the big leagues, Gates Brown and I both went up there to speak to the inmates. We got up on a platform out in the yard and had a little question-and-answer session with them, the same way Billy Martin and Frank Howard did when I was in prison.

I don't mind going back there. I still have a lot of friends on the inside. If seeing me gives them a reason to hope, a reason to think, if I could do it, maybe they can make something out of themselves, too, I'm glad to do it. Besides, when I walk through those front gates now, I know I can turn around and walk right back out any time I want to.

I've remained close to my parents. They're very pleased with the way my life has changed, and I've tried to help them as much as I could. When I began playing baseball my mother assumed I was going to make a lot of money right away and expected too much. I had to explain that my first responsibility was to myself and my own family. But as long as I'm playing baseball, as long as I'm living, I don't want my parents to have to worry about anything.

I don't blame them for my having gone bad. I blame myself. My father no longer drinks and I'm proud of him for that. I'm closer to him now than I ever was. We have a great relationship.

I also have a great relationship with Deborah. I bought a small house for us so that she'd have a place to call her own. She has talked about getting married, but I'm not ready for that yet. Maybe, eventually, I will be. Meanwhile I have given my daughter LaRonda my last name, and I'm looking forward to watching her grow up.

I'd like to help raise my brother Gerald's little boy, too. At three he's an intelligent kid, and I don't want to see his mind go to waste. The LeFlore family has suffered a lot; there's no reason for that suffering to continue. My mother has lost two sons and seen me sent to prison; I don't know if she could stand to see her grandson's life ruined, too.

I enjoy kids. When I get out of baseball I hope to be a coach or a counselor or to work with kids in some other capacity. I'm involved in the Police Athletic League in Detroit, trying to give kids some direction, some discipline, so they won't make the mistakes I made. Maybe just talking to me will help some of them straighten out.

One day I spoke to a group of teenagers at a juvenile detention center on Detroit's west side, and I could tell they were thinking about the same things I was thinking about when I was their age.

"I'm not going to tell you what to do," I said, "because I'm not the person to do that.

"I am going to tell you one thing. If you get caught using drugs or stealing, you're going to go to prison, just like I did. But don't get the idea you'll be as lucky as I was. There won't be a major league baseball team waiting to sign you when you get out. Just because it happened to me; don't you expect a miracle, too."

Epilogue

Although Ron seldom returns to his old neighborhood—which has gone downhill, if that's conceivable, since he departed—he remains a hero to those living there who remember him or have merely heard of him.

When he walks down the street, past the supermarket he robbed more than once and the ice cream stand where he worked until he was caught stealing, people stop to shake his hand and slap him on the back and wish him well. Those passing in cars recognize him and honk their horns, or wave to him out their windows.

He is a symbol even amidst all that squalor. He made it, he's a success, but he's still one of them.

The same is true inside the intimidating walls of Jackson Prison. On his occasional visits, Ron is hailed as a hero who has returned. His athletic exploits in prison are, to this day, the standards by which the inmates measure their own achievements. And his success with the Tigers is closely monitored, even by those prisoners who never knew him.

His boyhood friend, Calvin Qualls, who once regarded Ron as sort of a big brother, readily admits he still looks up to him. And he's not alone.

"A lot of people in the neighborhood remember him and look up to him," said Qualls. "We talk about him all the time.

"I'll see a guy on the street and mention the fact that I've seen Ronald and before we know it, we'll have talked for two hours about him. It's just that easy to do.

"I'll be sitting in a bar and the baseball scores will come on TV, and right away the guys will start talking about Ronald."

All his life, Ron has wanted people to look up to him. As the best thief, as the best fighter, as the best at whatever he happened to be doing.

Privately Ron yearns for the day when reporters talk to him about baseball instead of about the time he spent behind bars; the day when he's recognized as Ron LeFlore, a ballplayer who happened to be an ex-con, rather than LeFlore, an ex-con who happened to be a ballplayer.

Index